Perspectives on the Ideas of Gregory Bateson, Ecological Intelligence, and Educational Reforms

C.A. BOWERS

with chapters by
Rolf Jucker, Jorge Ishizawa and Grimaldo Rengifo

Eco-Justice Press, LLC
Eugene, Oregon, USA

Printed in the United States of America

Eco-Justice Press, L.L.C.
P.O. Box 5409
Eugene, OR 97405
www.ecojusticepress.com

Cover artwork: Morris Graves (1910–2001) American
"Bird in Moonlight," 1939, Gouache and watercolor on paper
Nancy Wilson-Ross Collection; Jordan Schnitzer Museum of Art; 1986:115
Used with permission from the Morris Graves Foundation

Text design: Lynn Marx

Library of Congress Control Number: 2011923173
ISBN 0-9660370-0-6

Perspectives on the Ideas of Gregory Bateson, Ecological Intelligence, and Educational Reforms | with chapters by Rolf Jucker, Jorge Ishizawa and Grimaldo Rengifo. By C.A. Bowers

Also by C.A. Bowers

Contents

CHAPTER 1

Introduction

Understanding the core ideas of Gregory Bateson will help to clarify how many of the current approaches to educational reform are based on ecologically destructive cultural assumptions. His critique of these assumptions, which have their roots in the abstract and thus culturally uninformed theories of western thinkers, also provides a way of reconceptualizing how educational reforms can foster an ecological rather than individually centered intelligence. The former is practiced in many non-western cultures, and even in our daily lives. Learning to exercise ecological intelligence in more aspects of daily life, given the nearly seven billion people who are adopting the western individually centered consumer-dependent lifestyle, will be absolutely essential if there is to be any hope of slowing the current rate of environmental destruction.

Before introducing Bateson's core ideas it is first necessary to provide an overview of the cultural (including political) context into which these reforms must be introduced. This will enable readers to recognize reasons to be optimistic that fundamental changes can be made, as well as the current ideas and traditions that will continue to be sources of resistance.

On the optimistic side are the multiple approaches now being taken to reduce the ecological footprint of humans. Governments are struggling with the double bind of protecting their economies, which are major contributors to the increasing rate of climate change, while at the same time searching for ways to scale back the amount of carbon dioxide being released into the atmosphere. Community groups are encouraging the wider use of bicycles, community gardens, barter systems, and even local currencies. Community activists are encouraging schools to introduce students to a more realistic understanding of the differences between local and industrially processed food. Local governments are even being challenged to change the laws prohibiting the raising of chickens in backyards, and to permit clothes lines in public view—which reflects the range of debate around how to live in more ecologically sustainable ways. Unfortunately, there are many sources of resistance to acknowledging that the climate and oceans are changing, and that millions of people are suffering from the effects of those changes.

The response to the environmental challenges by public schools and universities has been varied, ranging from the collaboration of environmentally oriented faculty and administrators to adopt more energy-efficient and carbon-reducing technologies to a small minority of faculty in the social sciences, humanities, and professional schools who are introducing environmental issues into their courses. Just as there are large segments of the public who deny that there is a growing ecological crisis, most faculty outside the sciences and such departments as architecture and urban planning continue to use the time-honored tradition of academic freedom to justify supporting the traditional lines of inquiry to which they were introduced in their own years of graduate study. While many faculty think of themselves as advancing the cutting edge of their field of inquiry, few recognize that their thinking is based on many of the same deep cultural assumptions that underlie the last two hundred or so years of forging the modern, industrially dependent and consumer-oriented form of consciousness that is now being globalized and pushing the world toward ecological catastrophe.

Efforts to introduce educational reforms that address how such abstract god-words as individualism, freedom, progress, free-markets, emancipation, etc., have marginalized awareness of environmental limits need to be based on a clear understanding that there is no public consensus about the nature of the ecological crisis—let alone that a crisis exists. What is occurring across the United States can best be described as political and moral chaos, ranging from the deepening cultural wars, the clash of regional economic interests, the stranglehold that corporations have on the legislative process in Congress, the Pentagon's agenda for safeguarding the global interests of corporations—which includes maintaining more than 700 bases in foreign countries—to extremist groups who now claim their individual sovereignty from all governmental laws and other responsibilities of citizenship. Other cultures rightly view the scale of national indebtedness in the United States as a growing sign of weakness.

The political discourse, which has become increasingly Orwellian, shows the same signs of political and moral chaos—with a growing populist movement that has little use for accurate information and the wisdom of an historical perspective. Indeed, the demagogues who now skillfully use the media have become the new sources of political and moral leadership for millions of Americans. The current shredding of what remains of the national consensus on the importance of the Constitution, of the democratic process that is based on an educated citizenry, of addressing the unresolved patterns of economic and political discrimination, and of making the changes in personal lifestyles and modes of production and consumption needed to ensure the prospects of future generations, raises the equally important question of how the upcoming generation is being educated.

The culture of public school and university education is equally varied, ranging from an increasing reliance upon computer-mediated learning, a focus on raising test scores by adopting a national core curriculum, classroom teachers and professors forcing upon unsuspecting students their own professionally prescribed orthodoxies and ideologically driven interests that make up the patchwork of courses and personalities called a public school and university education, to efforts to introduce students to the history of prejudice directed toward minority groups, and to consider how to achieve a socially just society. There are also commonalities shared by these diverse trends. These include a view of language that precludes recognizing how words, as metaphors, reproduce the patterns of thinking, prejudices, and silences of earlier thinkers who were unaware of environmental limits. Also included is a core set of deep cultural assumptions that underlie the modern agenda of promoting greater individual autonomy, a scientifically and technologically based form of progress, and the ideological framework that encourages exploiting the cultural wealth of the world's diverse cultural commons by transforming them into the monetized form of wealth required by the industrial system of production and consumption.

Clearly, it might seem that encouraging educational reformers and others concerned about the cultural roots of the ecological crisis to take seriously the ideas of Gregory Bateson, especially those that challenge many of the conceptual orthodoxies passed along as part of a public school and university education, will be a hopeless undertaking. Yet, there are a growing number of individuals and groups who are exploring different local approaches to living less consumer-dependent lives and to revitalizing the intergenerational knowledge essential to the local cultural commons. The increasing rate of environmental change, and its adverse impact on hundreds of millions of people around the world, will inevitably increase the number of people who will be searching for local answers. Media accounts of environmental changes, ranging from extreme weather conditions to the melting of glaciers and changes in the chemistry of the world's oceans, will eventually get the attention of educational reformers and policy makers. Some state departments of education are now beginning to recommend that environmental education be taken more seriously. Even though they limit environmental education to the scientific study of how natural systems are being degraded and exclude an understanding of the cultural beliefs, values, and practices that are degrading natural systems, this small shift in focus is encouraging. While not overly optimistic about how quickly Bateson's ideas will be taken seriously, I think that over time educational reformers will turn away from the iconic reforms of the last century and begin to focus on the classroom reforms that are consistent with Bateson's core insights. Only by introducing his ideas in a more systematic manner, and making the connections between key ideas and actual classroom practices, will educational reformers address the cultural roots of the ecological crisis.

To sum up, a major focus of the book is on the need to promote ecological intelligence rather than continuing to reinforce the myth of individual intelligence. A second focus is on how print-based thinking and communication alters consciousness in ways that are profoundly different from that which develops in orally based cultures, with one of the major differences being how print-based thinking fosters abstract thinking and thus a lack of awareness of local environmental and cultural contexts. A third focus is on the languaging processes which are not adequately understood by educational reformers—which include how the meaning of words (metaphors) are framed by the analogs chosen by earlier thinkers who were unaware of environmental limits and how their own patterns of thinking were based on the deep cultural assumptions constituted even earlier in their culture's history.

Chapter 2, "Gregory Bateson's Contribution to Understanding Ecological Intelligence," introduces five key ideas that provide the conceptual framework for understanding the double binds that lead to reinforcing in public schools and universities the same patterns of thinking that are exacerbating the ecological crisis.

The five key ideas include:

1. The "differences which make a difference" that constitute the basic units of information that circulate and undergo transformation within both the cultural and natural systems;
2. The recursive nature of earlier misconceptions that continue to frame current ways of thinking;
3. The failure of "maps" (conceptual frameworks constituted in the past) to accurately represent the "territory" (everyday cultural and natural ecosystems);
4. The conceptual and moral double binds that prevent us from recognizing how supposed "progressive solutions" are actually deepening the crises; and
5. The need for educational reforms that promote "Level III thinking" which focuses on the ecologically problematic taken-for-granted cultural assumptions inherited from the distant past.

Also discussed are the cultural assumptions that classroom teachers and university professors continue to pass on to the next generation and how rectifying these misconceptions leads to reinforcing ecological intelligence.

Chapter 3, "An Ecological Intelligence Perspective on Social Justice," examines how current approaches to the educational reforms that address social justice issues are based on abstract and culturally uninformed assumptions about the individual being the basic social unit, change being an inherently progressive process, and the ongoing process of critical inquiry leading to emancipation from the past. That these assumptions do not take into account such important issues as how the silences within the current social justice discourse on educational reforms about the nature of the ecological crisis prevents consideration of how the increasingly degraded state of natural systems will have the greatest impact on already marginalized students. It is stressed that ignoring the nature of the ecological intelligence that is part of the intergenerational traditions of different ethnic minorities further undermines the ability of marginalized youth to avoid the further limitations on their life chances that will accompany the continued loss of meaningful work. The outsourcing and automation of the workplace are the realities that must be challenged, as well as finding alternatives to the deepening ecological crisis that is already increasing the cost of basic sources of protein and water. Bateson's concept of double bind thinking is clearly demonstrated by the educational reform proposals that further promote the emancipation of the individual when what should be reinforced is how to exercise ecological intelligence that strengthens forms of community self-sufficiency and mentoring relationships that reduce dependence upon consumerism.

Chapter 4, "The Democratic Nature of Ecological Intelligence," draws upon several of Bateson's key ideas to make the point that the myth of individual intelligence legitimates a highly abstract approach to democratic decision-making. That is, it leads to thinking that the highest expression of democracy is in voting for a politician who will represent one's interests at levels of decision-making that range from city hall to the state and federal government. Unfortunately, the political discourse which is supposed to lead to more informed decisions has now been corrupted by the media and ideologues, corporate interests, and an unwillingness to engage in dialog with people who have different values and political agendas.

An alternative way of thinking of the political process is to view the acts of the individual who exercises ecological intelligence as expressions of democratic decision-making. That is, democratic decision-making should be associated with using technologies that have a smaller ecological footprint, engaging in cultural commons activities that contribute to the self-reliance of local communities, developing skills that lead to producing something which is useful to others and is part of a locally oriented economy, and engaging in practices that do not further degrade the life-sustaining habitats of other species. In a more concrete and immediate way, the expression of these preferences legitimately can be viewed as voting for one set of values and outcomes over other possibilities. To paraphrase Michel Foucault, an action upon an action represents the micro-level of political action. His shorthand way of identifying the connections between the exercise of power (which may be culturally influenced in ways that are not recognized) and its impact on the Other (gene, plant, animal, person) is similar to what Bateson is getting at when he says that a "difference which makes a difference" is a basic bit of information that the Other responds to and then undergoes changes that circulate as further differences within the layered and interactive ecosystems. The exercise of democracy should now be understood as the ability of ecological intelligence to recognize and adjust behaviors to what contributes to the sustainability of the different levels of the complex cultural and natural ecosystems. This is the form of democracy in which the individual's actions (which are a form of voting) are not so easily corrupted by corporate money and by self-serving politicians who are less and less accountable to the people who vote for them.

Chapter 5, "How Ecological Intelligences Leads to Reframing the Origins of Moral Values," focuses on the differences between the widely held view that individuals base their moral values on a rational or emotive process and how the exercise of ecological intelligence involves an entirely different way of thinking about the origin of moral values. A few decades ago educational reformers were urging students to choose the values by which they wanted to live—a view that has been supported by more recent educational reformers who equate progress with critical thinking and thus emancipation from all traditions. Underlying this approach are the recursive patterns of thinking that represent the individual as autonomous—even in the area of moral values—and change as inherently progressive. The exercise of ecological intelligence, on the other hand, leads to a fundamental change in which awareness of local contexts, including patterns of interdependencies, reframes how moral values are understood. This involves a shift from the subjective interests of the supposedly autonomous individual to those that contribute to the life-renewing capacity of the natural systems—and to what strengthens relationships of mutual support within the community.

Bateson's insights about how our conceptual maps are inadequate guides for understanding the territory (the existing state of the cultural and natural ecosystems) are also the basis for presenting an alternative explanation of the origins of moral values. Instead of locating moral values in the rational and emotive choices of the individual, a more culturally grounded explanation is that moral values are constituted and intergenerationally passed along as part of the process of framing the meaning of metaphors by earlier generations. The meanings of words (metaphors) are framed by the choice of analogs, and the choice of analogs reflects the culture's understanding of the analogs' attributes. How those attributes are understood then becomes the basis of what constitutes morally permissible behavior. If the wilderness is understood as a source of danger, it becomes morally permissible to bring it under human control by turning it into an exploitable resource; a plant, if not *funny.* seen as having any useful attributes, is identified as a weed and thus in need of being exterminated with an herbicide. Similarly, the culturally prescribed characteristics of different groups of people—women, members of minority ethnic groups, elderly, handicapped, etc.—dictate different forms of discrimination as morally appropriate. Changes in how attributes are understood lead, in turn, to a change in the meaning of words (such as woman, wilderness, desert, etc.) and thus to a change in what is regarded as moral and immoral behaviors. In effect, moral values are passed along as part of the ecology of language that becomes the basis of thinking and moral judgment of later generations.

Chapter 6, "How the Classroom Uses of Computers Undermine Ecological Intelligence," identifies the different ways in which computers reinforce the myth of individual intelligence. The educational uses of computers are unable to make explicit Bateson's insights about the recursive nature of what is today assumed to be cutting-edge thinking, about the metaphorical basis of our conceptual maps, and about the ecology of the differences that circulate and change the behavior of organisms within the natural and cultural ecosystems. Other important educational issues include the way in which computers privilege sight over the other senses, and print over voice—both of which, according to Walter Ong, contribute to abstract thinking. Also explained is how the educational uses of computers reinforce a conduit view of language, and thus ignorance about the metaphorical language that reproduces the ecologically problematic misconceptions of earlier eras. Why computer-mediated learning cannot lead to what Bateson refers to as Level III thinking, which involves examining the culture's deepest taken-for-granted assumptions, is also considered. The educational use of computers can provide access to highly useful sources of information about changes occurring in natural systems, but this advantage is partly negated if the teacher is viewed as replaceable by computers—which is the current trend toward achieving greater economic efficiencies. Overlooked is that information about the nature of the ecological crisis is of little value if the cultural assumptions that continue to deepen the crisis are not examined—and only an informed teacher can raise questions and provide an historical perspective when the taken-for-granted cultural assumptions appear in what the students are reading and in the class conversations.

Chapter 7, "Educational Reforms that Foster Ecological Intelligence," summarizes the previous discussions of the differences between an ecological and an individually centered view of intelligence and then presents an overview of the pedagogical and curriculum reforms that foster ecological intelligence. Specific recommendations are listed under the categories of "Ways in Which Ecological Intelligence is Undermined," "Ways in Which Ecological Intelligence is Reinforced," "The Linguistic Colonization of the Present by the Past—and of Other Cultures," "Educational Reforms that Contribute to Revitalizing the Local Cultural Commons and to an Understanding of the Modern Forms of Enclosure," and "Understanding the Cultural Transforming Characteristics of Computer-Mediated Learning and Communication."

Most school teachers and university professors reinforce not only individual intelligence but also many of the same deep cultural assumptions (root metaphors) that underlie the industrial/consumer-oriented culture that is now being globalized. Thus, the specific recommendations for fostering ecological intelligence suggested here provide the conceptual framework that should guide the process of reforming teacher education and the equally difficult task of introducing ecologically sustainable thinking across the academic disciplines.

Other Perspectives on Ecological Intelligence

Chapter 8, "Is a Systemic Education Transcending the 'I' Even Imaginable? Some Reflections from German-Speaking Europe," by Rolf Jucker, director of the Swiss Foundation for Environmental Education, goes to the heart of the double bind that characterizes how the United Nations' Decade of Education for Sustainable Development (popularly known as ESD) is being interpreted by educators in Europe and other parts of the world. After comparing the dominant mode of thinking among the European middle classes (which is focused on economic growth) with Bateson's conceptual framework for understanding the life-sustaining characteristics of ecological intelligence, Jucker examines whether European educators writing on how to implement the UN mandate for ESD question the economic growth paradigm. An examination of current books written on how to translate ESD reforms into classroom practices led him to conclude that there is a general unwillingness on the part of educational reformers to question the dominant economic growth paradigm. He also found a lack of questioning about the increasing reliance upon the educational uses of computer technology.

Even more problematic is how the educational proponents of ESD in Europe promote a constructivist view of learning. Constructivism, as Jucker notes, promotes the most extreme form of individualism as well as the idea of unlimited freedom. As he points out, both are based upon abstract theories that ignore the differences in how cultures intergenerationally renew themselves—that is, how learning is inescapably rooted in the languaging processes of different cultures. Drawing upon his previous writings, Jucker also explains how the constructivist view of learning fails to take account of the basic reality of all human existence; namely, that living a life in accordance with the myth of unlimited freedom and the individual's subjective construction of reality lead to behaviors that will not survive the collapse of life-sustaining ecosystems. The crux of the double bind is that the western cultural assumptions that underlie the idea that students should construct their own knowledge and values continue to be major contributors to the deepening ecological crisis—and that the European educators have not awakened to this reality.

Chapter 9, "Revitalizing the Ecological Intelligence of Andean Amazonian Communities: The Way Back to Respect," is written by Jorge Ishizawa and Grimaldo Rengifo, co-directors of the Proyecto Andino de Tecnologías Campesinas (PRATEC). Their use of the phrases "colonizing gaze" and "revitalization of ecological intelligence" brings into focus the tensions between the historical European-American approaches to exploiting the resources of the Peruvian Andes and the recent efforts of PRATEC to revitalize the ecological intelligence that has been practiced by local Andean communities for centuries. Ishizawa and Rengifo provide an historical sketch of the role that PRATEC plays in nurturing the recovery of the complex traditions of ritual, the ability to read the signs of natural processes (what Bateson refers to as the differences which make a difference) and to adapt agricultural practices to what the signs are communicating about when and where the fields should be planted. In addition to explaining how the cosmovision of Andean cultures is the basis of the practice of the "ecological governance" of life-sustaining practices, Ishizawa and Rengifo focus on the differences in approaches to education.

In following the western model, the universities in Peru continue to promote the industrial approach to agricultural practices while ignoring the depth of indigenous knowledge of how to sustain the biodiversity in different regions of the Andes. PRATEC's approach to supporting the local NGOs that work with communities has led to the emergence of alternative community-centered approaches to passing on the ecological wisdom of how to nurture the environment, which as they understand, also nurtures them. Modeled on the idea of the Mexican Earth University, what is called "UniVida" in Peru has no formal curriculum or other institutional characteristics of the western-style university. Rather, it provides the space where community members, old and young, meet to learn from each other the skills and practices best suited to the local environmental conditions. To date, three "schools" have been organized under the umbrella of UniVida. These schools provide youth and members of the community the opportunity to share the community's accumulated knowledge relating to biodiversity and food sufficiency, crafts and skills, and for intercultural dialogue—which also introduces youth to an understanding of the forces shaping globalization and of the rights of indigenous peoples.

Gregory Bateson's Contribution to Understanding Ecological Intelligence

The challenge facing educators is far more complex than merely providing students with the data connected with the scientific findings about changes in the earth's ecosystems. It is also more complex than educating them in how to develop new technologies that are less disruptive to natural systems. As the late Gregory Bateson warns, our survival depends upon a radical transformation of the dominant patterns of thinking in the West. These patterns are widely shared, passed along in everyday conversations, and encoded in the built culture. The institutions that give special legitimacy to these patterns of thinking are the public schools and universities. They have the greatest potential for providing the conceptual space necessary for understanding the historical roots of the misconceptions underlying the myth that if humans rely upon rational thought they can control the changes occurring in natural systems. They also are the sites where students can learn about the nature of ecological intelligence and how the exercise of ecological intelligence leads to correcting the destructive impacts of earlier assumptions and practices on natural systems and human communities. One of Bateson's key insights about the recursive nature of cultural belief systems reminds us that past ways of thinking, both in terms of the conceptual history of the culture as well as the conceptual history of the professor, are likely to be ignored—thus dooming to failure the efforts to correct the conceptual errors of the past.

Before discussing the fundamental differences between the dominant view of individual intelligence (including the cultural assumptions that support it) and the nature of ecological intelligence, a brief sketch of Gregory Bateson's background would be useful. He was born into the family of a prominent British biologist in 1904 and died in 1980. He began as a student of zoology but quickly shifted to the field of anthropology—which led to his fieldwork in New Guinea where he collaborated with Margaret Mead, whom he eventually married and later divorced. According to his own account, his first book, *Naven*, contained his initial insights about the hidden influences on the observer's perceptions and analyses. Following his move to the United States, Bateson began to work in the field of psychotherapy and to participate in the early discussions of cybernetics. Both fields led to important developments in his understanding of the connections between communication processes and what he refers to as the double binds in human and human-and-nature relationships that perpetuate the problems rather than solving them. His last two books, *Steps to an Ecology of Mind* (1972) and *Mind and Nature* (1979), are now recognized as his most important contributions. The former, which is the most widely read, is a collection of essays and printed versions of talks he gave to various audiences. As in nearly all cases where radically new ideas are presented to groups that are encountering them for the first time, the introduction to key ideas and themes tends to be repeated in different sections of the book. The elaboration on certain key ideas, as well as Bateson's arguments with counter points of view require book-length treatment—which can be found in Peter Harries-Jones' excellent book, *A Recursive Vision: Ecological Understanding and Gregory Bateson* (1995).

My purpose here is to introduce several of Bateson's more fundamental ideas and to explain how they lead to rethinking both the idea of individual intelligence and the cultural assumptions that support it. I also explain how his insights are the basis for understanding ecological intelligence, as well as their practical implications for introducing educational reforms that do not rely upon the past misconceptions that are major contributors to putting our culture on an ecologically destructive pathway. While I introduce several ideas from Bateson's other writings, the clearest account of his insights can be found in the sub-section of his chapter on "The Cybernetics of 'Self': A Theory of Alcoholism" (1972, pp. 309–337). The sub-section is titled "The Epistemology of Cybernetics" and is a mere six pages in length. The challenge will be to expand upon his short explanations in a way that enables the reader to recognize how they transform our traditional individually centered understanding of how we acquire knowledge, engage in relationships with others and the environment, and begin to make the transition to an ecological way of thinking. First, I will present a summary of the different ways in which individualism and the supporting cultural patterns are part of the experience of most Westerners. There are, of course, variations in how this sense of individualism is experienced. Differences can be traced to the influence of local cultural traditions, ideologies, religions, and what has been learned from personal experience.

Summary of Assumptions Underlying Being an Autonomous Individual

The personal pronouns "I," "me," and "you," as well as the names we are given set us apart from others, and continually reinforce the sense of being an autonomous individual. This culturally mediated experience is further reinforced by the cultural tradition that emphasizes sight over the other senses as the most accurate way of acquiring knowledge—which reinforces the sense of being separate from the object observed. This leads to the subjective experience of having a unique perspective on events in the external world. The conduit view of language (which I have written about elsewhere) and the idea of objective knowledge promoted by the intellectual class also marginalize the awareness of the cultural and environmental influences that must be ignored if the myth of being an autonomous individual is to be sustained. Taken-for-granted cultural assumptions required to support this myth include the ideas that change is a linear form of progress and that this is a human-centered universe. Also reinforcing the idea of individualism are the Enlightenment assumptions about the power of rational thought. Today, Enlightenment thinkers and their followers have contributed to the widespread cultural amnesia by framing the meaning of the word "tradition" in a way that has reduced it to whatever is associated with maintaining privileges, backwardness, and oppressive practices. The myth of progress, and the increased reliance upon computers which reinforces the idea that the individual is in control of where in cyberspace she/he wants to explore, further adds to a state of awareness that makes traditions appear as irrelevant. In addition to the tradition of civil liberties, which George Lakoff wrongly identifies with progressive thinking, there are overwhelming economic and technological forces that further strengthen the special status that individualism has in western cultures. These include market liberalism, as it equates the expansion of capitalism with the expansion of individual freedom, and libertarianism, as a more extreme ideology that celebrates the "Virtue of Selfishness"—which is the title of one of Ayn Rand's books.

The special status given to print-based technologies, such as books and computers, while having many positive and essential benefits, also reinforces abstract thinking and the individual's ability to exercise critical thought. Critical thinking has led to challenging many sources of oppression and has clearly contributed to important achievements in the area of social justice. However, a more complex understanding of the many uses of critical thinking will reveal that it is also used by special interest groups who are working to overturn government regulation of exploitative practices, and to manipulate public opinion in order to gain support for foreign wars that benefit corporations and the military personnel's need for steady advancement through the ranks. Critical thinking is essential to developing new strategies for manipulating the public's consumer addiction and its willingness to support a bloated military budget. Advertising agencies and various extremist groups also rely on critical thinking to develop their strategies, as do social justice groups—albeit for radically different purposes.

There are cultural traditions that have not been completely marginalized by these various emphases on individualism. The traditions of the natural and cultural commons, while under threat by market forces, now are undergoing renewed support by members of local communities where mutually supportive values and interests are recognized as giving meaning to what is too often the autonomous individual's sense of isolation and lack of meaningful purpose. Other individuals who are working to improve the quality of everyday life by strengthening the community's infrastructure of roads and public services are finding, to quote the title of Robert Putnam and Lewis Feldstein's book, that life is "better together." They are an example of the civic individualism mentioned earlier. These groups, as well as religious groups trying to live by the moral guidelines of the Social Gospel, are motivated by a connected sense of individualism that goes against the grain of market liberal and libertarian thinking. Social justice advocates and environmentalists also have political and moral agendas that differ radically from the larger segment of the population that places self-interest and reliance upon what they assume are their own ideas above all else.

A public school and university education is another powerful force that contributes to the myth of being an autonomous individual—or at least having the capacity to achieve this highest expression of human self-realization. Classroom teachers and university professors have adopted a number of strategies for convincing students that they are account-able for having their own ideas and values. Educators reinforce this mes-sage by encouraging students to create their own values, to identify what careers they want to pursue, and to rely upon the wealth of information and data available on the computer for developing their own ideas. At the university level, students are expected to cite the source of ideas that they have not originated. The irony is that this expectation is supported by not informing students about how the language they rely upon to express their "own" ideas is actually metaphorical in nature and thus carries forward the prejudices and silences that were the basis of the taken-for-granted patterns of thinking of earlier generations. Included in the misconceptions reinforced by most faculty are the ideas that the rational process is free of cultural influences, that there is such a thing as objective interpretations, information, and data—and that abstract knowledge is more reliable than what is passed along through face-to-face communication and, generally, oral traditions. The curriculum in most institutions of higher education mirrors that of a supermarket, where individual choice maximizes the appeal of a university education and also has a powerful influence on the students' sense of being autono-mous, self-directed agents. The connections between the ways in which individualism is reinforced, and the actual culturally mediated embodied experience of the student, are too complex to be fully addressed here. Nevertheless, this overview is adequate for highlighting why these vari-ous expressions of individualism inhibit the development of ecological intelligence. It is also adequate for recognizing why Bateson's ideas lead to a radically different, and indeed more accurate, understanding of human/nature relationships than the explanations provided by the con-ceptual and moral mainstream western cultures.

Bateson's Insights about the Nature of Ecological Intelligence

Any discussion of Bateson's core ideas is likely to be met with an im-mediate response of incomprehension and frustration, especially for the reader who has become accustomed to ideas being reduced to little more than sound bites. The following statements, which appear in the six short pages I suggest as providing the best overall introduction, turn out to be two of his most profound insights. They will be more fully explained as we go more deeply into Bateson's other key ideas. Espe-cially important is his statement: "A 'bit' of information is definable as a difference which makes a difference. Such a difference, as it travels and undergoes successive transformation in a circuit, is an elementary idea." (1972, p. 315)

As we shall see, this statement about differences being the basis of the information networks we more conventionally know as an ecology is also critical to understanding the following:

> The total self-corrective unit which processes information, or, as I say, 'thinks' and 'acts' and 'decides,' is a *system* whose boundaries do not at all coincide with the boundaries either of the body or of what is popularly called the 'self' or 'consciousness'; and it is important to notice that there are *multiple* differences between the *thinking system* and the 'self' as popularly conceived. (1972, p. 319)

The question that might arise in trying to make sense of these two statements is: How did Bateson's education lead him so far astray? And his response would likely be the question: How did the West fail to recognize that it was making a major epistemological error when it emphasized things as separate entities? In the following statement he corrects what he regards as this basic mistake in thinking: "...while I can know nothing about any individual thing by itself, I can know something about the *relations between things*." (1987, p. 157)

Part of the answer to why things rather than the relations between things has become a dominant pattern of thinking in the West can be attributed to the privileging of a print-based form of consciousness over that of oral/narrative-based cultures. Plato, according to Eric Havelock, played an important part in this transition, which had the effect, along with many important benefits, of marginalizing the importance of contexts. Without an awareness of contexts the printed word takes on the role of referring to things—which is an abstraction just as the use of the personal pronoun "I" is an abstraction. Individuals, plants, animals, rivers, geological formations, etc., can be represented in terms of their physical characteristics, and even in terms of their behaviors. But this leads to a highly restrictive understanding, one that largely omits the formative relationships and interactive patterns within the larger ecology. Print allows for explanations of causality, but even these represent the writer's interpretation of relationships. The myth of objectivity helps to hide the imposition of the author's interpretation, which may be framed by cultural assumptions of which she/he is seldom aware. These assumptions, in turn, go far back into the past of the language community.

Contemporary examples of this cultural proclivity to think of things as distinct entities rather than the formative influence of their relationships (or what can be referred to as the ecology of which they are a part) can be seen in the way species from other parts of the world have been introduced into different regions of North America—with disastrous consequences for native species. Fields, rivers, forests, and even backyards are now undergoing dramatic changes as native species are being crowded out. This cultural emphasis on separate entities, rather than on formative relationships, can also be seen in how a worker is defined in terms of a salary, a student in terms of a grade, a product in terms of the price put on it—and the way in which an individual's identity can be reduced to a social security number. As David Goleman documents in his book, *Ecological Intelligence* (2009), understanding a product in terms of its life cycle assessment—that is, its production history which includes the use of chemicals, toxins released into the environment, the amount of energy required, the patterns of labor, and the ecological footprint connected with its recycling—represents an alternative to the long tradition of thinking of things in terms of distinct entities. Similarly, in the past the student's grade was assumed to be an expression of her/his intellectual achievement, but recently there is a greater emphasis on considering the formative relations that may be responsible for the student's level of performance. There are many other examples where things are no longer understood in isolation from their surroundings—that is, the larger ecology of relationships in which they participate. Nevertheless, print-based knowledge continues to marginalize contexts, and tacit understanding continues to perpetuate the emphasis on "things," as does our daily practice of relying upon nouns and pronouns rather than verbs.

Equally important are several other ideas that differ radically from the dominant way of thinking in the West—and are critical to understanding Bateson's statement that differences are elementary ideas and sources of information, and that the unit that processes information is much broader and more inclusive than the thinking individual. These include the ideas of recursion, that the map is not the territory, the nature of double bind thinking, that human intelligence and action do not occur as processes separate from the information circulating through the relationships that make up the system, and that in systems that show mental characteristics no part can exert unilateral control over the whole.

Each of these ideas needs to be integrated so that they are understood as part of a larger system of ecological intelligence. Ways of thinking that depart from ecological intelligence, as Bateson puts it, lead to an ecology of bad ideas that threatens the system as a whole. Each of these ideas is essential to how Bateson understands the ecology of mind. Introducing each idea separately also makes it possible to identify how thinking of intelligence as one of the distinguishing attributes of the autonomous individual limits her/his awareness of how embodied experiences are nested in larger information networks.

The Many Faces of Recursion
—And the One Most Related to Ecological Intelligence

Recursive patterns of thinking exist in a variety of areas—including mathematics, computer science, and in a culture's ways of knowing—or what Bateson refers to as a "recursive epistemology." The focus here will be on understanding what he means by a recursive epistemology and what this phenomenon helps us understand about why educators continue to reinforce the ecologically uninformed patterns of thinking that have their roots in earlier mythopoetic narratives (including the writings of major western philosophers) and powerful evocative experiences—including experiences shaped by technologies mistakenly thought of as neutral "tools."

As in so much of Bateson's writings, ideas are seldom presented in a straightforward manner where the reader obtains what might be considered a final definition and not a further engagement with the ideas of other theorists. The possibility of a workable definition is often sacrificed by Bateson's own qualifications as he rethinks his own insights—and how far they can be generalized. The following list both presents a key feature of Bateson's understanding of recursiveness in the culture/language/thought process, as well as the difficulty of penetrating his conceptual process. In a collection of essays edited by his daughter, Mary Catherine Bateson, and published under the title, *Angels Fear: Toward an Epistemology of the Sacred* (1987), Bateson presents an explanation of recursion as a characteristic of structure, which he extends to the epistemological structure of a cultural way of knowing.

1. 'Structure' is an *informational* idea and therefore has its place throughout the whole of biology in the widest sense, from the

organization within the virus particle to the phenomena studied by cultural anthropologists.

2. In biology, many regularities are part of—contribute to—their own determination. This *recursiveness* is close to the root of the notion of 'structure.'

3. The information or injunction which I call 'structure' is always *at one remove from its referent*. It is the name, for example, of some characteristic immanent in the referent, or, more precisely, it is the name or description of some relation ideally immanent in the referent.

4. Human languages—especially perhaps those of the West—are peculiar in giving undue emphasis to Separate Things. The emphasis is not upon the relations between but upon the ends of relationship, the relata. This emphasis makes it difficult to keep clearly in mind that the word 'structure' is reserved for discussion of *relations* (especially to be avoided is the plural use 'structures').

5. Insofar as the name is never the thing named and the map is never the territory, '*structure*' is never '*true*.' (1987, p. 161)

Peter Harries-Jones summarized one of the ways in which Bateson's understanding of recursion can be understood: "Recursion as a process of continuous looping [is] a process without observable attributes of structure" (1995, p. 187). The metaphor of "looping" is useful here as it suggests that life-forming and sustaining processes, including life-threatening processes, do not move in the linear direction modern thinkers associate with progress. To stay with Bateson's example, the original conceptual structure that leads to the use of language, and thus to the pattern of thinking that is finely attuned to naming things rather than relations and contexts, is further reinforced when this pattern of thinking is exercised today. To make the point more directly, the conceptual structures (or what I refer elsewhere to as the root metaphors) formed in the past continue to influence the present, and the present loops back to reinforce the conceptual structures formed in the past. For example, the root metaphor of mechanism introduced by Johannes Kepler and other scientists—which enabled them to think of phenomena in terms of measurement, experimentation, and innovation—has become reified and today is the conceptual model for understanding a wide range of processes, including the human brain, the genetic engineering of seeds, and behavior modification.

Other root metaphors inherited from the past continue to frame how people think today—including their use of vocabulary, shared silences, and explanations of causal relationships. These different examples of recursion exist as part of the collective and tacit memory of the culture. Because Bateson often explains recursion by using the concept of a thermostat to make his point about the looping or feedback of information in a self-perpetuating system, some readers have mistakenly assumed that he is promoting a mechanistic way of thinking. This has led to overlooking the more important implications of understanding cultures as recursive systems. Also overlooked is that he is identifying one of the key reasons that we continue to rely upon the same metaphorical language to extricate ourselves from the ecological crisis to which this language contributed.

There are two key insights that Bateson brings to our attention: one being that we take for granted the conceptual structures rooted in the distant past and continually reinforced through the thought patterns of succeeding generations. The other insight is that today's tendency to associate change with linear progress is a cultural construction that loops back and repeats the earlier symbolic structure that came into existence when Enlightenment thinkers interpreted the emergence of modern sciences and a technological form of consciousness, literacy, the idea that rational thought should replace traditions, and the idea that humans were not only given the power to name the participants in the natural world but also to exploit them for their own purposes.

Bateson does not ignore other aspects of the West's recursive cultural epistemology. His criticisms include all the characteristics of modern consciousness that can be traced back to the earliest mytho-poetic narratives that focused attention on the abstract religious debates about what follows the death of the individual rather than on learning from the behavior of the natural systems upon which people depend. Other recursive patterns underlying modern consciousness include powerful evocative experiences, such as organizing daily life in accordance with the rhythms of a mechanical clock and the many ways of representing and justifying a linear view of progress. Many of Bateson's most direct and explicit criticisms are directed at the Cartesian view of the individual that represents thinking and awareness as separate from the world of interacting relationships.

Among the recursive patterns classroom teachers reinforce is the idea that individuals have the power to originate their own ideas. This is reinforced when the teacher asks: What do *you* think? What do *you* see (where it is assumed that the student has a unique vantage point on the external world)? What do *you* want to happen? Who do *you* want to become as an adult? And so forth. The emphasis on nurturing the student's creativity, experimentation, and even achieving the fullest expression of freedom by rewriting the ends of traditional stories in ways more in line with what the student values and wants to happen, are all common examples of what is reinforced in classrooms—especially in the earliest grades. The recent emphasis on students constructing their own ideas, relying increasingly upon computers as a way of accessing abstract information, explanations, and simulations, and now the addiction of students to communicating through cell phones and text messaging, all reinforce the view of the individual who, as Descartes announced, possesses the power to exercise rational thought that is free of the influence of traditions. This is, of course, an illusion promoted by progressive-oriented cultural forces that too often have given legitimacy to replacing the non-monetized traditions with reliance upon consuming goods and services. However, unlike the Santa Claus illusion, most people never wake up to the reality of how many daily traditions they rely upon.

The irony is that while some classroom teachers are encouraging students to be more conscious about relying upon local sources of food and engaging in recycling, they are still reinforcing the abstraction that represents the individual as autonomous—or at least has the potential to become so. Even the more ecologically informed approaches taken in environmental education classes fail to challenge the Cartesian misconception that represents the individual as an independent observer of phenomena occurring in the local streams and other environmental sites. To give this criticism greater credibility, one has only to look at the failure of teachers of environmental education to introduce students to the idea that the words they use have a history, and that these words—such as progress, technology, community, science, and so forth—involve the recursive process of repeating the same silences and misconceptions of earlier thinkers who also took for granted the conceptual structures of their culture and era.

With the major exceptions being in the sciences that have taken an ecological turn, most university faculty also reinforce the idea of the student as an autonomous entity who is responsible for making explicit the distinction between her/his own ideas and those derived from outside authorities. Also reinforced is the use of personal pronouns that reinforce the myth of individual autonomy, as well as the emphasis on objective knowledge that hides the influence of the languaging processes that reproduce the recursive interpretive frameworks currently taken for granted or expressed in the new vocabulary of critical thinkers. The result is that most students graduate from colleges and universities thinking of language as a conduit in a sender/receiver process of communication and that what is shared in this sender/receiver process of communication are their own thoughts and values. Few are aware that their use of language and their thoughts repeat the earlier deep patterns of thinking formed before there was an awareness that many non-western cultures had prioritized the importance of understanding relations within natural systems and had developed an ecological form of intelligence, an awareness that there are environmental limits, and an awareness that the printed word is profoundly different from the living nature of the spoken word.

Just as the public school teacher who continually recycles the myth of linear progress as a way of justifying an individually centered view of intelligence, most university graduates also take for granted this cognitive pattern ("structure" in Bateson's language) and thus give legitimacy to a misconception that J.B. Bury traces back to the Enlightenment thinkers who assumed that reliance on the rational process and experimental inquiry were cumulative and thus guaranteed progress into an infinite future (1932). Unfortunately, myth was seen as having been banished by the power of science, technology, and rational thought. Yet, there are many examples where myth continues to influence the development and use of modern technologies. For instance, the accumulated knowledge in the field of chemistry, which has led to natural systems (including the human body) being impacted by thousands of synthetic substances, such as DDT, PCBs, and dioxins, was all initially understood as breakthroughs and celebrated as further examples of progress. Knowledge in other high-status fields of inquiry that most westerners associate with a linear form of progress are now being discovered to be ecologically problematic—yet the ways in which language perpetuates this recursive process continue to go largely unnoticed.

Bateson's reliance on the process of recursion to explain how we unknowingly perpetuate the misconceptions of the past leads to another basic insight that has particular importance for educational reformers. This insight was borrowed, as Bateson acknowledges, from Alfred Korzybski, a Polish-American philosopher and scientist. Bateson sums it up with the phrase "the map is not the territory."

The Map Is Not the Territory: How the Metaphorical Nature of Language Misrepresents the Differences Which Make a Difference

Bateson recalled the time when he arrived at the insight that enabled him to make the connection between Korzybski's distinction between map and territory and the epistemological issues he was working through. It was in 1970 while he was preparing his talk for the Korzybski Memorial Lecture. In response to the question he asked himself, "What gets from the territory onto the map?" the answer became clear that, as he put it, "News of difference is what gets across, and nothing else" (1991, p. 188). The connection Bateson made between Korzybski's now famous phrase and his own insight about what represents the most basic unit of information that undergoes constant transformation while circulating through all levels of the earth's eco-systems may appear quite mystifying.

Bateson was attempting to resolve the problem of the relationship between the mind and the external world—a problem that is ignored by nearly all public school teachers and most university professors even though their task is to provide the conceptual frameworks that will guide how students think about the external world, as well as their internal world. In elaborating further on the mind/external-world relationships, Bateson makes a further observation that is fundamental to recognizing the conceptual error that dominates education in the West. Following a restatement that what gets from the outside world into the brain is *"news of difference,"* he goes on to make the following observation: "If there is no difference in the territory, there will be nothing to say on the map, which will remain blank. And, further, I saw that any given map has rules about what differences in the territory shall be reported on the map." (1991, p. 200)

Map and territory are metaphors. The "map" refers to the cultural/metaphorical language/thought connections, while the "territory" is the world of the natural and cultural systems we commonly refer to as the environment in which we live. An especially important part of Bateson's statement about maps (a culture's way of knowing) is that they contain the interpretative frameworks that govern which differences which make a difference will be recognized and how they will be understood. For example, if only the increase in profits is given attention when growing genetically modified seeds, the differences which make a difference that signal environmental damage will go unnoticed. Similarly, focusing only on the loss of employment may lead to ignoring the carbon dioxide an industry is releasing into the atmosphere, which is contributing to changes in the ocean's chemistry. What Bateson is getting at in this statement about how cultural rules influence what will be recognized and how they will be interpreted is the role that the deep assumptions of the culture (root metaphors) play in framing what we are aware of as well as what will be ignored. To reiterate an important point: These cultural assumptions are largely taken for granted, thus leading to the process of selective awareness and interpretation that will be experienced as a natural, rather than as a cultural, construction.

The question that is likely to arise is: What does Bateson mean by saying that the differences which make a difference are the basic units of information, and why does he suggest that when differences are not present we have nothing to respond to? First, we need to clarify what he means by the statement that "a 'bit' of information is definable as a difference that makes a difference. Such a difference, as it travels and undergoes successive transformation in a circuit, is an elementary idea." (1972, p. 315) What he does not mean is that the "elementary idea" is like the metaphorical representation of ideas. Rather, it is the information that is processed at various levels—genetic, chemical, energy, behavior, thinking, etc.—that leads to a change in the organism or system that can process the way in which information is coded. For example, the introduction of toxic chemicals during the development of the fetus may represent a difference which makes a difference in terms of chromosomal damage that becomes, in turn, a difference which makes a difference in the development of the immune system—which then leads to a chain of differences that results in a variety of physical problems that then become a lifetime of differences which make a difference for the child, parents, and various social agencies. In this example the information communicated through differences circulates through interdependent systems where differences in the chemistry of an industrial process lead to differences in the functions of genes—and eventually to differences at the cultural level.

The introduction of a non-native plant starts another cycle of differences which make a difference. That is, when the chemistry of insects, including pollinators, does not fit with the chemistry of the non-native plant, differences which make a difference circulate through the local ecology—affecting the native plants that rely upon the bees and other insects essential to the pollination process, as well as the birds that rely upon the insects and the other participants in the local food chain. Bateson's seemingly simple phrase encompasses the information exchanges that support the self-development processes of every organism in an ecosystem as well as provide the sources of energy that are shared. When the different sources of energy are lost or changed, another complex set of differences circulates through the interdependent systems. Bateson is challenging the western idea that only humans are intelligent and can process information when he states that differences are sources of information and "an elementary idea." Ecosystems also process information *True* in ways that are often beyond what humans can understand or replicate. What the dominant western epistemology fails to understand is that the natural environment is not reducible to matter and blind forces. Rather, it is sustained by the different ways in which "differences" are processed, and this is dependent upon eons of genetic development within different environmental contexts.

For Bateson, the maps are the metaphorical constructions that provide the interpretive and moral frameworks of the culture. What is important about the map/territory metaphor is that the map is rooted in an earlier cognitive/mythopoetic history. That is, the meanings of *Interesting* words (metaphors) are framed by people who are successful in having the *& true* analog they selected accepted by others, and even by later generations. Furthermore, their process of analogic thinking is framed by the taken-for-granted root metaphors of earlier times. In terms of the West, these root metaphors include patriarchy, anthropocentrism, mechanism, progress, individualism, economism, and now evolution—with ecology becoming a new totalizing interpretive framework which is challenging the earlier root metaphors that underlie the industrial/consumer-oriented culture. These root metaphors, or "cognitive structures," are the recursive epistemologies that are taken for granted today. They also underlie the process of linguistic colonization as Westerners attempt to force other cultures to base their daily lives on these root metaphors.

To state the problem more directly:

1. The metaphorical maps are generally out of date—that is, the long-established metaphorical language relied upon to respond to changes circulating through both the natural and cultural message systems contributes to the lack of recognition of what is most critical to slowing the rate of environmental degradation and the increase in social injustice.

2. The modern western-influenced maps, when relied upon by cultures existing in different bioregions, distort awareness of the interdependence between the local culture and the natural systems that needs to be taken into account if the rate of environmental degradation is to be reduced. For example, the cultures in the Peruvian and Bolivian Andes are unlikely to reduce the catastrophic consequences that lie immediately ahead (where the key difference which makes a difference is the melting of the glaciers that are the source of their water) if they rely upon the conceptual maps borrowed from the western cultures for guiding how they are to live—as these maps are major contributors to global warming.

3. The root and image metaphors need to be continually revised in order to limit even greater human suffering and environmental damage. Updating the maps requires being aware of the differences in the first place. This is not the old problem of what came first, the chicken or the egg—especially when it is understood that updating the maps upon which the next generation relies requires that classroom teachers and university professors be aware that there is an ecological crisis. They also need to recognize that science and technology alone will not help to mitigate the crisis, and that there are cultural traditions (recursive patterns) that are deepening the crisis. Solutions other than technological fixes are especially needed and will introduce students to community-centered and mutually supportive lifestyles that are less dependent upon consumerism and the industrial model that is based on a money economy and the pursuit of profits.

The Problem of Double Bind Thinking

The issues discussed up to this point—recursive looping where the present repeats the conceptual patterns and errors of the past, and the problem of conceptual maps that are outdated and of the wrong territories—represent different aspects of double bind thinking. Many of Bateson's original comments on the nature of double bind thinking were intended to clarify the abnormal communicative patterns of schizophrenics, as well as communication problems in general. However, what is most pertinent here are his views on how double bind thinking prevents us from moving beyond the recursive pull of basic misunderstandings of human/nature interdependencies. Peter Harries-Jones quotes how Bateson understood the connections of double bind thinking and the ecological crisis: "All communicative activity should be considered as a set of propositions about the world or the self, whose validity depends on the subject's belief in them. It [is] these beliefs *about* the world that should be the major topic of investigation." Harries-Jones further notes that "double bind, in Bateson's view, was never a matter of simple intellectual confusion or of being caught in a dilemma of 'I am damned if I do and I am damned if I don't.'" The double bind, for Bateson, involves "a situation in which simple dilemmas [are] compounded by falsified contexts, supported by patterns of interpersonal communication which ensured continuation of the denial that a falsified context [exists]." (1995, p. 135)

A falsified context can take many forms, such as the lack of awareness of the cultural construction of different interpretations of reality. Apathy and indifference toward exposing the reifications that lead people to take for granted that the interpretations are accurate representations of "reality" are yet other examples of a falsified context. The most prevalent examples of a falsified context involve relying upon a system of knowing borrowed from the distant past and used as a guide for understanding today's world, and thus representing language as being free of historical and cultural influences. Again quoting Harries-Jones, Bateson associates double bind thinking "with some combination of denial and inflexibility derived from the cultural predisposition about the salience of rationality and rejection of holism." Bateson is very specific about the nature of this inflexibility when he notes in one of his letters that "as long as the West remains tormented by a false pride in individualism, it will pursue perversions of individualistic thinking. This tormented perspective," he continues, "can lead to strategies in which killing the whole biosphere becomes preferable to risking one's own skin." (Harries-Jones, 1995, p. 227)

Really? [handwritten marginal note]

The Unit of Intelligence Is the Individual Plus the Immediate Differences Which Make a Difference—Plus the Recursive Cultural Epistemology that the Individual Takes for Granted

Bateson's challenge to the modern idea of individual intelligence has many dimensions. Included in the earlier quotation in which he refers to the "total self-corrective unit" are three key points:

1. Thinking, or what is generally referred to as the exercise of intelligence, is not like a process that leads to an idea that is like a photograph—such as a mental image in which the boundaries are clearly framed off from the local contexts. Rather, Bateson refers to processing information in a way that involves continual self-correction and adjustments as differences which make a difference are taken into account.

2. Processing the elementary (and non-metaphorical) idea or information undergoing transformation as it circulates through the system occurs even when the individual is not involved. As Bateson puts it, "there are multiple differences between the *thinking system* and the 'self' as popularly conceived" (1972, p. 319, italics added). That is, the metaphor of intelligence needs to be expanded in ways that take account of the different ways in which information is coded and intergenerationally passed along.

3. The way the individual processes information is not always aligned with the cognitive/moral epistemology she/he inherits from the past. The individual may engage in self-correcting behavioral and reflective responses, while still taking for granted the reified ideas of an earlier time. Awareness of gender bias seldom involves recognizing the reified ideas of linear progress and a human-centered world. That is, the individual's reified ideas continue to perpetuate the state of self-denial—even as behaviors are undergoing changes in response to the differences circulating through the different pathways of information exchange that make up the larger ecology.

I think we are definitely in this kind of stage. [handwritten marginal note]

The question may arise about the classroom teachers and university professors who reinforce the idea that students are autonomous thinkers who are responsible for constructing their own ideas. This view of human intelligence carries with it the moral obligation in the West of citing from whom ideas are borrowed—or being deemed guilty of plagiarism. Or, is Bateson correct when he claims that the unit of intelligence (which he treats as a verb) is the individual, plus information circulating through the natural systems, plus the cultural epistemology that was constituted in the past and encoded in the languaging processes, plus the intergenerational legacy acquired as part of the taken-for-granted stock of knowledge? In *Steps to an Ecology of Mind,* Bateson uses the following example to highlight what is missing in the western view of individual intelligence. The example also highlights the interconnections between intelligence and the difference which makes a difference.

> Consider a man felling a tree with an axe. Each stroke of the axe is modified or corrected, according to the shape of the cut face of the tree left by the previous stroke. The self-corrective (i.e., mental) process is brought about by a total system, tree-eyes-brain-muscles-axe-stroke-tree; and it is this total system that has the characteristics of immanent mind. (1972, p. 317)

Other examples where the exercise of intelligence can be seen as participatory—and including the information flowing through the life-sustaining pathways of the larger system within which the individual is embedded—can be seen in the processes of non-verbal communication. A change in tone of voice, facial expression, or even a lengthy pause in a conversation, leads the person who is aware of the differences which make a difference to alter both behavior and thinking—which, in turn, leads to altering the response of the other person. Indeed, the adjustments take account of the response to what was previously said as well as the behavioral cues that accompanied what was said. The traditional farmer who is making a decision about when and where to plant a crop also exercises intelligence in a way that is influenced by the information circulating through the different interacting ecosystems of soil, plants, weather, quality of seeds from last year's harvest, and so forth. If the reader has had experience in sailing a boat, she/he will recognize that the decisions about the adjustment of the sail and rudder are continually modified in terms of the differences which make a difference in the water/wind ecology. Changes in the color of the water often signal a change in the velocity of the wind. The size of the waves and the direction of the current also influence the degree of heeling of the boat, and the change in tack always takes account of the direction of the wind as well as where one hopes to arrive. Life in the natural environment is also affected by differences which make a difference. Gary Snyder puts it this way: "The world is watching: One cannot walk through a meadow or forest without a ripple of report spreading out from one's passage. The thrush darts back, the jay squalls, a beetle scuttles under the grasses, and the signal is passed along. Every creature knows when a hawk is cruising or a human is strolling. The information passed through the system is intelligence." (1990, p. 19)

All of the above examples involve giving careful attention to relationships. Changes in the cut face of the tree, the non-verbal patterns of communication of the person with whom one is engaged in conversation, the soil that is to be planted, and the course that is to be sailed, could be (and too often are) erroneously thought of as separate things, entities, and objectives. When the interactive relationships are ignored, the exercise of intelligence becomes formulaic and a preconceived strategy is put into play. When this occurs, the information circulating within the natural and cultural systems becomes ignored, with attention being given to what the individual has been culturally conditioned to be aware. That is, the old conceptual maps take over, with the individual's awareness being limited primarily to what the misconceptions of earlier thinkers bring into focus. For example, today's market liberals, whose focus on achieving greater profits is guided by the abstract theories of classical liberal thinkers, do not consider the differences which make a difference in the cultural and natural ecologies in which they are embedded. This leads them to ignore the differences introduced by their actions, such as increased levels of poverty, deskilling of workers, increases in toxic pollution, damage to the self-renewal of natural systems, and so forth. That is, if they were educated in a manner that reinforced the importance of giving attention to relationships—rather than rigidly being guided by the abstract free-market ideology—perhaps they would recognize another point that Bateson makes. Namely, that "in no system which shows mental characteristics can any part have unilateral control over the whole. In other words, *the mental characteristics of the system are immanent, not in some part, but in the system as a whole*." (1972, p. 316)

This statement relates directly to the moral values that should be integral to the exercise of ecological intelligence. The epistemological shift from focusing on things to relationships also involves a shift in the role that language plays in carrying forward the culture's moral templates. Metaphorical thinking, which is framed by the analogs settled upon by earlier thinkers, carries forward how they understood the attributes of things, such as trees, wilderness, the ocean and rivers, non-native plants, animals, and so forth. For example, when wilderness was understood as a source of danger, it was both rational and moral to treat it as an exploitable resource. Similarly, plants not considered to have any useful attributes were called weeds and in need of being eradicated. One of the attributes of the oceans, namely their vastness, led to thinking of them as impervious to human impact and thus moral responsibility. Because insects were thought to be lacking in useful attributes, exterminating them with a pesticide was a morally appropriate behavior. Root metaphors, such as anthropocentrism and progress, provided moral legitimacy for introducing into the environment thousands of synthetic chemicals that we are only now recognizing as part of the emerging health catastrophe that is the legacy of early and current scientists. The root metaphor that represented the world as a collection of things, which included autonomous individuals, framed how earlier thinkers understood the attributes of things that ranged from women, indigenous peoples, pre-literate cultures, and so forth. Reducing them to things rather than recognizing their relationships within their cultural and natural ecologies, which would have led to a more complex understanding, made it easier to label each as possessing only a negative attribute—which, in turn, made it unnecessary to be morally accountable toward them.

Bateson's emphasis on understanding ecosystems as layered, interactive, and interdependent self-renewing systems, ranging from genes to cultural assumptions, leads to a shift in how moral values are to be understood. He recognizes that in some systems the relationships are disruptive and thus are ecologies that are not likely to survive. He refers to them as an ecology of weeds and bad ideas. One of these bad ideas is that humans, by relying upon the rational process and new technologies, will be able to survive the destruction of natural systems. In a passage that recalls his criticism of the West's recursive epistemology which continues to separate the fate of humans from the fate of the environment, he issues the following warning:

> The environment will seem to be yours to exploit. Your survival unit will be you and your folks or conspecifics against the environment of other social units, other races, and the brutes and vegetables. If this is your estimate of your relation to nature *and you have an advanced technology*, your likelihood of survival will be that of a snowball in hell. You will die either of the toxic by-products of your

own hate, or, simply, of over-population and overgrazing. The raw materials of the world are finite. (1972, p. 462)

Following this passage, Bateson goes on to say that the most important task today is to learn to think in a new way. Before considering what he describes as the three levels of learning, and how the latter level leads to what can be called ecological intelligence, it would be useful to address a response that both philosophers and educational theorists are likely to make. Because Bateson appears at first glance to be a process thinker, they are likely to associate his ideas with those of John Dewey. This would be a major mistake, and for the following reasons.

Basic Differences Between the Ideas of Gregory Bateson and John Dewey

On the surface there appear to be many similarities between Bateson and Dewey. Both understand that knowledge has to be continually revised in order to take account of a constantly changing world. A second surface similarity is that both reject the idea that intelligence is an attribute of the autonomous individual. For Dewey, intelligence involves problem solving in a democratic context which becomes more efficient as communication with others is enhanced. The argument that Dewey was an early environmental thinker, which would suggest another favorable comparison with Bateson, is based on interpreting Dewey's understanding of intelligence as an integral part of experience—and experience as part of the natural world. This view of intelligence avoids the error inherent in the Cartesian mind/body separation of which Bateson is also critical.

Given these surface similarities between Dewey and Bateson, educational reformers who have recently recognized that there is an ecological crisis, and who are searching for a conceptual framework that will guide their thinking, are likely to feel that their years of relying upon Dewey's progressive and democratically oriented theory of knowledge make it unnecessary to take on the challenge of understanding Bateson's admittedly difficult vocabulary and concepts. However, if these reformers were to examine the differences in any depth, they will recognize that Dewey, for all of his useful insights, is part of the problem. Let me cite the following as evidence. First, Dewey grew up during successive waves of environmental devastation, such as the killing off of millions of bison, the clear-cutting of forests across the country, the destruction of prairie grasses—not to mention his support of the industrial processes that were spewing billions of tons of carbon dioxide and other toxic chemicals into the rivers and into the atmosphere. He says nothing about the environmental destruction of his era. In fact, while he wanted democratic socialism to replace capitalism, he also thought that the growth and successes of the industrial culture would lead to wider acceptance of the scientific and experimentally oriented approach to knowledge.

Second, during his most formative intellectual years, the indigenous cultures were being decimated, by some estimates, to 90 percent of their previous population. Their lands were being taken over by the Anglo/Euro-Americans, and Dewey remained silent. His understanding of the indigenous cultures, which exhibited many of the characteristics of ecological intelligence, is summed up in several books in which he describes them as having the thought patterns of "savages." Dewey's racism has been defended on the grounds that he shared many of the taken-for-granted prejudices of his era. This seems a weak excuse, especially in today's world when there is an increasing awareness of the connections between linguistic diversity and preserving biodiversity. There is another aspect of Dewey's thinking about other cultural ways of knowing, which he lumps together under the category of "spectator knowledge," that makes his theory of knowledge and the educational reforms derived from it especially problematic. He does not represent instrumental experimental inquiry as just one of many approaches to knowledge. Rather, it is the only legitimate approach. Dewey's colonizing mentality leads to reducing all forms of knowledge to three categories: savage, spectator, and experimental inquiry. These categories represent Dewey's way of understanding the stages of social progress. He was, like other intellectuals of his era, a Social Darwinian thinker who was driven by the idea that if the educational process teaches students the importance of participatory decision-making in solving problems by using the scientific mode of experimental inquiry, they will be able to escape the intellectual prisons of their immigrant parents. For Dewey, there is only one valid approach to knowledge, and this approach requires overturning the traditions of intergenerational knowledge that sustains the cultural commons of these diverse immigrant groups.

A criticism that can be made of Dewey, which is the same one that Bateson makes of scientists, is that Dewey was not a reflexive thinker.

His assumptions about the progressive nature of experimental and participatory problem solving led him to ignore the deep cultural assumptions that led to his silence about the environmental devastation and the threat that the industrial model of production and consumption posed for the environment and other cultures, as well as the ecological knowledge of the indigenous cultures he labeled as savages. While Edward Sapir and Benjamin Lee Whorf were beginning to explore the connections between language, ways of knowing, and cultural practices, Dewey remained indifferent to the reality constituting role of language—particularly how the metaphorical thinking of earlier eras carries forward their misconceptions and silences. Friedrich Nietzsche was writing about this problem in the 1880s, so it would be unfair to excuse Dewey for being unaware of the cultural/metaphorical language issues that are receiving such wide attention today. The important point is that today's followers of Dewey reproduce in their own thinking about educational reforms the same silences that resulted from Dewey's lack of reflexive thinking.

Bateson avoids adopting any of the prejudices that characterize Dewey's thinking. Indeed, it is difficult to find any reference to Dewey in Bateson's writings, just as it is difficult to find in Dewey's writings any reference to ecology—even though the word was widely used in the early 1900s to refer to the study of natural systems. My suggestion, in light of the rate of changes taking place in the earth's ecosystems, is that thinking about the educational reforms that contribute to an ecologically sustainable future should focus on developing a deeper understanding of ecological intelligence—including Bateson's contribution to understanding the double binds that inhibit the educational reforms that foster ecological intelligence. Dewey can be credited with introducing educational reforms during an era of rote learning and childhood repression, but these reforms are now widely accepted. It is time for his followers to begin addressing reforms that foster lifestyles and patterns of thinking that are less damaging to the environment. Among these reforms are lifestyle changes that do not fit with Dewey's emphasis on continual change and experimentation—which he associated with progress in moving beyond the non-scientifically grounded traditions of the past.

Exercising Ecological Intelligence and Level III Learning

A good place for starting this transition from the recursive epistemology of ecologically problematic ideas is by following Bateson's suggestion that we need to move beyond what he calls Learning I and II, by participating in Learning III. In an essay on learning written in 1964 and revised in 1971 for inclusion in *Steps to an Ecology of Mind*, Bateson summarizes the scientific research on Learning I and II. Learning I is limited to responding to a stimulus and then correcting the choice being made when given a set of alternatives. This is the form of learning observed in studies of rat behavior. Learning II involves a more complex set of responses, such as being aware of changes in the context within which choices are made. It also includes a range of attitudes that influence the process of learning. These include being fatalistic (e.g., accepting a given set of relationships and possibilities), an inability to question the otherwise tacit understandings of relationships and contexts, adopting an attitude of dominance or submissiveness that closes off recognition of other possible relationships and ways of thinking, and adopting a pattern of thinking where events are understood to be discrete rather than interconnected. To this list can be added learning within the limits established by reified beliefs and traditions.

If we translate the list of characteristics associated with Learning II into more contemporary language, it then can be understood as the ability to learn in contexts dominated by the expectation that events are beyond human intervention, that the culture's beliefs and values are taken for granted (which means that their cultural origins will not be recognized), that one's sense of authority and right to dominate others is absolute (either derived from God or a reified ideology), and that events are to be judged without consideration of their antecedents or future consequences. This level of learning is likely to ignore that others may have different interpretations and even different belief systems. Other characteristics include a willingness to accept the authority of the printed word and abstract knowledge, especially when they help to give legitimacy to ideas and values that the individual claims to originate. In short, Learning II can be seen in the cognitive style of the authoritarian personality. It can also be seen in the cognitive style of the indifferent and passive individual who seeks strength in following social conventions—even those that serve the interests of authoritarian individuals. Both types, and the many individuals who are both authoritarian in some areas and who find strength in belonging to emotionally charged mass movements, view themselves as individuals who are not dependent upon either culture or the natural environment. Their sense of autonomy leads to their thinking that they have no responsibilities except for what serves their personal interests or that of their immediate family.

That people engaged in Learning II are not the only ones existing in society led Bateson to consider the characteristics of people who exhibit Learning III characteristics. These are the characteristics that are essential for moving from an individually centered intelligence (Learning II) to that of ecological intelligence. Among the qualities Bateson associates with Learning III are:

1. An ability to question the premises underlying both one's own be-havior as well as practices and policies that govern society;
2. A willingness and conceptual ability to question what is taken for granted by Learning II individuals, and to introduce changes;
3. An awareness of the importance of understanding differences in cultural contexts;
4. An ability to assess habits (whether personal or culturally shared) in terms of whether they need to be revised, changed completely, or conserved, such as conserving habeas corpus and other civil liber-ties, as well as those aspects of the cultural commons that reduce dependence upon a market economy; and
5. An awareness of cultural continuities and interdependencies in both cultural and natural ecologies—and of the conceptual double binds that put the well-being of both at risk.

These characteristics are mutually supportive, and if taken seriously would lead to profound reforms in both public schools and universities. Bateson recognizes the difficulty in making the transition to Learning III, so the question might come up as to why we should persist in recom-mending reforms in the two institutions that most people operating at the Learning III level regard as tradition-bound—even as these institu-tions appear on the cutting edge of promoting even more extreme forms of modernism. (I use the word "tradition-bound," instead of "conserva-tive," as the latter is chronically misused in today's political discourse. Throughout the book, the argument is made that the exercise of mindful conservatism and ecological intelligence are essential to maintaining the cultural commons.)

If public schools and universities are continuing to reinforce the same deep cultural patterns of thinking that gave conceptual direction to the consumer/industrial culture that is now being globalized, even as some professors are working on new technological solutions, why argue that attention should be focused on reforming the modernizing traditions of public schools and universities? If we keep in mind that one of the principal characteristics of Learning III is the ability to question the premises upon which the taken-for-granted cultural practices are based, it quickly becomes obvious that there are few institutions in the mainstream culture where the underlying premises (what I prefer to call "cultural assumptions" and "root metaphors") can be questioned without facing personal, economic, and political consequences. Many families will not allow the assumptions that guide their economic, political, and moral decisions to be questioned and revised, and there are few other social organizations and institutions that would welcome this sort of questioning. The list includes most churches, community organizations such as the local city club and chamber of commerce, the Rotary Club and other civic organizations, National Guard gatherings, local sailing clubs and other sporting groups, gun clubs, places of employment—indeed, the list goes on and on.

I have serious reservations about whether most classroom teachers and university professors possess the conceptual background necessary for recognizing why many of the taken-for-granted cultural assumptions that underlie their academic discipline are ecologically problematic, or the willingness to take the ecological crisis seriously enough to begin questioning these assumptions. Nevertheless, public schools and universities are the two institutions that provide what can be called the psychosocial moratorium necessary for raising difficult questions and obtaining an historical perspective on how, in the name of progress, intellectual elites have succeeded in poisoning much of the environment, and in promoting a form of individualism that equates a level of consumerism that is ecologically unsustainable with personal happiness and success. While public schools have no tradition of academic freedom, they nevertheless can provide students with the initial conceptual basis for making the transition to exercising ecological intelligence without embroiling the school in controversy. The tradition of academic freedom is well established for universities, which allows for a more far-reaching examination of the guiding assumptions of the dominant culture. Thus, universities have the fullest potential for providing the conceptual space necessary for students to move to Learning III and to exercising ecological intelligence.

The task in the following chapters is to examine the differences between individual and ecological intelligence for how we think about social justice issues, the prospects of democracy, and the moral values that will guide our relationships as we enter an era of scarcity of water, protein, and habitable land. We will then turn to consider the current traditions in teacher education that must be taken into account before taking on the challenge of identifying the educational reforms that can be put into practice. This will involve examining how the educational uses of computers promote abstract thinking while marginalizing awareness of local contexts and the differences which make a difference in cultural and natural systems. Also to be considered is how the education section of UNESCO is promoting reforms in teacher education that are based on the double bind thinking of equating critical thinking and the individual construction of knowledge with educating for sustainable development. The last chapter will focus on how the Quechua of the Peruvian Andes have maintained their traditional practices of ecological intelligence.

CHAPTER 3

An Ecological Intelligence Perspective on Social Justice

There are daily situations when each of us exercises one or more of the characteristics of ecological intelligence. It may occur when we recognize that we are being labeled and thus stereotyped by the language others are using—which relates to Bateson's point about how the language/thought patterns that originated in the past continue to control the present thinking in ways that misrepresent current relationships and what is distinct about our own lives. It also may occur when we realize that the loss of employment or the break-up of a marriage is the difference which makes a difference that will be followed by a series of differences that require close attention if financial and other forms of disaster are to be avoided. Narratives that carry forward genuine moral insight, such as Martin Luther King Jr.'s "I Have a Dream" speech and Aldo Leopold's summary of a land ethic, bring to awareness that the unit of intelligence we need to exercise is the same as pursuing the common good. And there are times when everyone has questioned the taken-for-granted assumptions that have led to living in a way that is now undergoing a radical change. It is becoming more common for social reformers to think in terms of systems and to trace their origins back to earlier misconceptions, exploitive practices, and prejudices.

For individuals and cultures that live more on the margins, ecological intelligence has been central to survival. That is, they have to ensure that their conceptual maps are continually adjusted in ways that take account of changes in the environment, in the cycles of the plants and animals they depend upon, and in how their actions affect the other members of their group. In effect, they understood that the information circulating through the interdependent systems, as well as their own dependencies within these systems, is the unit of intelligence —and that their existence will be short-lived if they rely upon abstract ideas rather than an ability to interpret and respond to the changes in the ongoing relationships—which are the differences which make a difference.

The problem, however, is that the cultural traditions in the West, as well as the mix of cultural traditions that now characterize the modern world, seldom allow for all aspects of ecological intelligence to be a fully integrated part of daily experience. The ways in which the embodied experience of the individual, regardless of her/his cultural traditions, is culturally mediated and largely taken for granted means that the recursive nature of the culture's way of knowing will remain largely unrecognized. This results in a disconnect between the conceptual maps upon which daily life is based and the rapid changes occurring in the cultural/natural environments. An example is the experience of many adults not feeling at home in the emerging global cyber-culture. The current effort to give every young student in the world a computer further promotes the epistemological characteristics of cyber-culture that are at the root of this new generational divide. This not only contributes to the loss of ecological intelligence among subsistence cultures but also reinforces the western traditions that represent the individual as autonomous, and that language is a neutral conduit in a sender/receiver process of sharing "objective" information, data, and the individual's subjective ideas.

Discussing the connections between current ways of thinking about social justice and the need to make the transition from individual to ecological intelligence requires a certain leap of imagination—a leap that allows us to think that it is possible to make the transition to ecological intelligence—which will require another leap to a place where we can move beyond hope to the reality of learning to adapt our core patterns of thinking in ways that do not degrade further the life-sustaining characteristics of natural systems. The following discussion of how the practice of ecological intelligence leads to the reframing of how we understand social justice issues, and the reforms that need to be implemented, is intended as part of the argument for understanding why developing our capacity to exercise ecological survival depends upon what Bateson refers to as Level III learning. It is also intended to clarify how the exercise of ecological intelligence leads to a fundamentally transformative way of thinking about social justice.

The Problem of Defining Social Justice in a Multi-Cultural and Politically Diverse Society

How social justice is understood varies among individuals, who are each influenced by a wide range of differences in their primary culture's way of knowing and value system. For liberal classroom teachers and professors, social justice issues continue to be defined in terms of the economic and political marginalization of groups that fall into the categories of race, gender, and social class. As these teachers and professors are largely from the middle class, or are aspiring to become members of the middle class, the social and educational reforms they promote involve providing access to the forms of education that will enable marginalized students to earn *True* a living that will raise them above the poverty level. Other educational goals include enabling these students to participate on more equal terms in the democratic process, to live in safe neighborhoods and in adequate houses, and to join the middle class in pursuing the American dream of ascending the ladder of material progress. In short, the goal of liberal educational reformers is to improve the quality of life for individuals born into impoverished situations, and who are marginalized because of their gender, their skin color, or the low social status of their ethnic group. These are indeed important goals.

Other cultural traditions of thinking make the question of how to address social justice issues more complex and difficult to address. These diverse cultural orientations vary widely, ranging from the ethnic traditions brought from the homeland and religious traditions that mark certain groups and behaviors as undeserving of the cultural wealth that would enable them to escape poverty and other forms of discrimination, to ideologies that designate who should be the winners and losers in the struggle to survive. For example, the continuing influence of Calvinist thinking within certain Christian denominations leads to identifying the accumulation of material wealth as a sign of whom God favors. If all forms of work are understood as part of God's plan for sorting out those who deserve salvation (Colossians 3:23), then the individuals and groups not included in God's plan of predestination (the unemployed, the under-educated, those lacking in individual competitiveness, etc.,) deserve no special government support to compensate for what social reformers (being mere humans) consider to be the systemic reasons for the existence of poverty. For people still under the influence of this theology, poverty and discrimination are thus the result of personal failures, while economic success is evidence of being chosen by God for special blessings. Given this recursive conceptual/moral framework, what is required of educational reformers is to prepare the deserving for a life of economic success, and to leave the less deserving to fend for themselves.

Market liberals (free-market fundamentalists) and libertarian followers of Ayn Rand also rely upon a recursive conceptual/moral framework that reproduces the assumptions underlying the abstract theories of such western philosophers as Plato, John Locke, René Descartes, Adam Smith, and such Social Darwinian thinkers as Herbert Spencer and Leo Strauss. The idea of organizing society on the basis of free markets (capitalism), which Ayn Rand claims is a goal yet to be achieved (1964, p. 33), is winning wider acceptance among the public. The renewal of interest in Rand's writings gives further support to the market liberal's fundamentalist idea that the freedom of the individual is restricted by all forms of government interventions, including those aimed at eradicating poverty and creating greater equality of opportunity. What she calls the "objectivist ethic" is the individual's moral right to "act for his own rational self-interest" (p. 25). That she is part of the western tradition that relies upon abstract thinking for understanding social relationships and individual freedom can be seen in her interpretation of the rational process that guides a life of selfishness. As she puts it, "The selfishness or unselfishness of an action is to be determined objectively: it is not determined by the *feelings* of the person who acts. Just as feelings are not a tool of cognition, *so they are not a criterion in ethics.*" (p. 68)

What she wrote in the late fifties and through the sixties is like symbolic manna for the market liberal think tanks, such as the CATO and American Enterprise Institutes, for the CEOs of the corporate culture who promote capitalism throughout the world, and for the members of Congress and the Supreme Court who frame social justice issues in a way that supports both the religious fundamentalists, who are still in the grip of Calvinist theology, and the market liberal followers of Adam Smith, who transformed the local experience of markets into the universal principle of markets free of governmental regulation. Using slogans and writing in a reductionist style that easily translates into formulaic thinking, she declares that "it is capitalism that gave mankind its first steps toward freedom and a rational way of life" (1964, p. 151). If members of the public were educated to think at Bateson's Level III, they would become aware that their fear of falling from the middle class and even becoming homeless is not due to the government's regulation of capitalism and its efforts to provide support systems for the poor but can be traced to the failure to question the abstract ideas that underlie the mal-distribution of wealth in society. They would, in effect, understand the recursive patterns of thinking that now obstruct efforts to ensure that all members of society have a right to the food, health care, housing, and educational experiences essential to living to one's fullest potential.

With the large numbers of Americans who have been educated in the nation's public schools and universities now looking for political and moral leadership from media demagogues, such as Rush Limbaugh and Glenn Beck, as well as from pundits who are spokespersons for the market liberal think tanks, it becomes necessary to ask about the misconceptions and silences that have been passed along by their classroom teachers and professors. Did their education reinforce the conduit view of language that is essential to thinking that words and ideas accurately represent an external reality—thus marginalizing the awareness that words (metaphors) and ideas have a history that carries forward the assumptions and misconceptions of earlier eras? Did their education reinforce the abstraction of being autonomous individuals who are responsible for their own ideas and values? Were they educated to think of themselves as existing in a human-centered world where the environment can be exploited in order to achieve endless material wealth and progress? (Even John Calvin resisted the folly of this way of thinking—read his statements on the environment in his *Institutes of Christian Religion*.) Were they educated to think that technological innovations, scientific advances, and market forces lead to a form of progress that has no victims and does not degrade environments? Did their education introduce them to the importance of the traditions of civil liberties and the reasons for the separation of governmental powers, as well as provide them with the knowledge necessary for exercising communicative competence in making informed decisions? Other questions could be asked about the education received by the segment of the American public that is being led down the slippery slope leading to the increasingly real possibility of a totalitarian future.

One of the double binds in which social-justice-oriented educational reformers are caught is that they are thinking as if they are autonomous individuals, which leads to ignoring the need to address the educational reforms raised by the above questions. Social justice liberals think in terms of marginalized groups, but the members of these groups, whether an ethnic minority or the economic underclass, are understood as individuals who happen to be part of a cultural heritage that has been set apart from the mainstream culture. Too often, the goal of these social justice educational reformers is to enable students to escape from the prejudicial and exploitive practices that limit full and equal participation in the dominant culture, which leads, in turn, to students being educationally prepared to compete in the consumer-oriented middle-class culture. These educational reformers are likely to ignore the double bind nature of their well-intentioned reform agenda, and thus to claim that this is an unfair criticism, as they often frame social justice issues within the context of multi-cultural education. They do not recognize the double bind because they have not yet understood that the deepening ecological crisis brings into question many of the basic assumptions that the dominant culture is based upon. In effect, they do not recognize the recursive conceptual patterns that were a taken-for-granted part of their own education.

Unfortunately, while appearing to be a positive step forward, social justice education too often leaves ethnic minority students without a comparative understanding of the intergenerational traditions of knowledge, skills, and mutually supportive relationships that are core features of their own cultural commons and the consumer/market culture to which they have been denied full access. Some faculty who teach these courses may be members of an ethnic minority; others come from a white, middle-class background. While many ethnically grounded social justice faculty promote a knowledge of students' own cultural roots, they do not always help students understand the forces of enclosure that will force them to become increasingly dependent upon the consumer-oriented lifestyle within the dominant culture. That the classroom efforts to revitalize the students' ethnic traditions (cultural commons) do not automatically lead to an awareness of the forces undermining their traditional cultural commons was clearly evident at a recent conference held in Ontario, Canada. The elders of the major indigenous cultures in the area made a special effort to introduce the participants to their ceremonial cultural commons but were critical of the main purpose of the conference—which was to examine how the values, patterns of thinking, and technologies of the dominant culture were enclosing the cultural commons of the ethnic cultures. The elders failed to understand that the word "commons" was not being used as a way of marginalizing their traditions, but rather, as a term that refers to the intergenerational knowledge and skills, which differ from culture to culture, that have not been monetized and integrated into the capitalist system of production and consumption. If ethnic social justice faculty do not understand the nature of the cultural commons and the many ways in which they are being enclosed (that is, being integrated into the consumer and individually centered culture) their students will have only a limited understanding of the forces that continue to marginalize their ethnic traditions as well as threaten their prospects in the dominant culture. For example, how many ethnic social justice professors engage students in the process of making explicit the ways in which reliance upon various forms of electronic media undermine the face-to-face patterns of communication essential to passing on the intergenerational knowledge and skills that strengthen community self-reliance and that have a smaller ecological footprint? How many of their students understand the cultural transforming nature of print-based knowledge and communication?

The social justice faculty who come from a middle-class background compensate for their lack of in-depth knowledge of the cultural traditions taken for granted within the ethnic cultures by promoting critical inquiry as the only valid approach to knowledge. Many forms of intergenerational knowledge and skills that historically were essential to an ethnic group's survival are overlooked entirely or subjected to critical inquiry which teachers too often represent as empowering students to replace their cultural traditions with a progressive way of thinking and being. Few of these teachers are aware that other groups, many of whom gain from the impoverishment of others, also rely upon critical inquiry when formulating their strategies for achieving their own political and economic goals. Indeed, basing one's life and politics on a rationally based selfishness, which the libertarians and market liberals advocate, requires exercising critical thought. Like the questions of what constitutes social justice and whose social agenda is to be achieved through the use of critical inquiry, each group makes its own claims—and backs these claims with narratives that are increasingly disconnected from the world in which we live.

Before considering how a culture that has made the transition to exercising ecological intelligence would understand social justice issues, and the approach that schools and universities can take in addressing them, it is necessary to examine what is being ignored by current liberal educational reformers. The *Handbook on Social Justice Education* (2000), edited by William Ayers, Therese Quinn, and David Stovall, is an invaluable resource for understanding how most reformers understand the different forms of social injustice, as well as how classroom teachers should adapt their pedagogy and curricular decisions in ways that help to overcome the systemic roots of social injustice faced by many students.

At the outset, I want to emphasize that my criticisms of what is being ignored by the authors of the chapters on the nine categories of social injustice that are to be rectified by classroom teachers and university professors should not diminish the value of many of their recommendations. What needs to be focused upon here are the three areas of silence that are especially problematic. The silences and misconceptions in the thinking of these social justice educators remind us again of the importance of Bateson's observation about the recursive nature of a culture's guiding epistemology.

First Criticism

This 774-page tome contains only one reference to "ecological analysis," and there it focuses on patterns of human interaction—not on the cultural and natural system ecologies. The phrase "ecological crisis" only appears in one sentence, and there it is among the usual list of unresolved social problems. Given that Wal-Mart as well as other major contributors to a hyper-consumer, toxic-producing lifestyle are attempting to lighten their ecological footprint, and the plethora of books addressing both the nature of the ecological crisis and ways that local communities are working to recover their traditions of mutual support and self-reliance, the reader might expect that social justice issues would be understood in a more current way. There is now a huge literature on the impact of water shortages being experienced as a result of climate change, and it would seem that this would be seen as a critical social justice issue. In the United States alone, twenty percent of the population does not have access to clean water. Worldwide, more people are currently dying from the lack of potable water than are being killed in wars. The range of toxins that is affecting the development of children, as well as the illnesses experienced throughout society from the thousands of synthetic chemicals used in manufacturing processes, have been the focus of attention since Rachel Carson's book, *Silent Spring* (now in its 27th edition), and the first Earth Day in 1970. Climate change is now recognized as responsible for the melting of ice fields that are the source of water for hundreds of millions of people, as well as the droughts that are forcing people to become environmental refugees. In the last few years extreme weather conditions in the United States have produced serious droughts as well as flooding conditions that have contributed to unemployment, changes in diets, and a further decline into poverty. Even more serious environmental changes are beginning to impact daily life. Scientists, for example, are documenting that the chemistry of the world's oceans is becoming more acidic and is having an adverse impact on the bottom of the food chain upon which fish stocks and humans depend. This, combined with over-fishing, has already led to the collapse of major fisheries in different regions of the world. If the shortage of fresh water does not lead to international conflicts, the lack of ocean sources of protein will.

One has to ask why these well-publicized changes have escaped the attention of the contributors to the *Handbook*. If they had given thought to the social justice issues that have been the focus of a wide range of national and international organizations, one might have expected a radical reconceptualization of the social justice issues that can be traced directly to the globalization of the western model of development. These are issues related to homelessness, disease, death, hunger, and the refugee status of millions that result in the loss of the ability to achieve one's most basic potential as a human being. How does one explain the silence on the part of the contributors to the *Handbook*? One possible explanation can be found in the long list of books cited at the end of each chapter. Most of the citations refer to articles and books written by colleagues who share a similar educational background. Few of the cited books are written by environmentalists, by scientists concerned with how our bodies and environments are being poisoned by our industrial/consumer-oriented lifestyle, or by community environmental activists.

Second Criticism

The contributors' recommendations for achieving social justice in nine areas fail to take account of the social injustices experienced by the majority of the world's population. This oversight is due to the failure to consider the human impact of the ecological crisis. References to the contributions and failures of past approaches to multicultural education, to the need to foster critical thinking and a transformative lifestyle, to anti-biases in curriculum materials and pedagogy, and to the need to create positive learning environments, are important. But the repetitiveness of these recommendations does not help the reader obtain an understanding of the curricular changes that can help alleviate poverty and that will provide the conceptual basis for exercising communicative competency in resisting the further commodification and monetization of the local cultural and environmental commons. Again, the social justice educators rely upon the formulaic prescriptions of the late twentieth century, which include more critical thinking and more expressions of concern about the plight of social groups and individuals who face myriad forms of injustice. These prescriptions do not translate into recommendations for how individual and community gardens can be promoted, how traditional technologies for preserving food can be passed along, how volunteerism and mentoring in a wide range of non-monetized and mutually supportive activities can be promoted, or how to enable students to recognize the differences between their experiences in the cultural commons and in the market-oriented culture that will lead to the development of the communicative competence necessary for resisting the further enclosure of what has not been monetized.

Given the spread of economic globalization, colonization to a western, individualistic, consumer-oriented lifestyle, and the unrelenting quest for new technologies and markets, one of the dominant features of the future will be scarcity—in access to protein, to potable water and water for agriculture, to sources of a dignified and community supporting livelihood, and to the intergenerational knowledge that has enabled many cultures to achieve a degree of self-reliance without destroying the bioregions upon which they depend. The double bind the world is facing is that the emphasis on material progress is leading to more forms of scarcity—including the loss of the intergenerational knowledge and skills that enable people to live less consumer-dependent lives.

Several of the *Handbook's* contributors focus on the systemic causes of social injustices and suggest that students should be engaged in a discussion of how to bring about needed changes. What they miss, however, is that students should also be encouraged to engage in auto-ethnographies of their local communities in order to identify the forms of intergenerational knowledge and skills that need to be renewed. Indeed, the possibility that critical inquiry should also lead to an awareness of what needs to be conserved goes unrecognized by the contributors to the *Handbook*. Traditions, such as the gains in civil liberties, as well as recent achievements by the labor, civil rights, feminist, and environmental movements—all essential to addressing unresolved social justice issues—need to be part of the curriculum. Passing this knowledge on to the next generation is part of the process of conserving important social justice gains. Social justice education, contrary to the impression left by some of the contributors to the *Handbook*, should not represent all traditions as being sources of oppression. The legacy of previous social justice struggles should be a part of the collective memory, as it provides evidence of the importance of collective action focused on the common good—a value that is increasingly marginalized in our consumer and technology-addicted culture.

Third Criticism

Since both the students who are victims of social injustice, as well as those students who will dedicate their lives to improving the prospects of others, will encounter mostly a middle-class, consumer-oriented curriculum that may include only shallow introductions to the cultures of minority groups, the following questions arise: Do the contributors to the *Handbook* provide guidance for recognizing how to reframe the analogs that are encoded in the vocabulary that students encounter in most areas of the curriculum? Will readers of the *Handbook* be able to recognize how the vocabulary in the curriculum serves as a form of linguistic colonization of the present by past thinkers who were unaware of environmental limits? Granted, social-justice-oriented educators are more likely to be aware of the linguistic colonization that goes on in multicultural classrooms. But they are unlikely to be aware of the history of the analogs that frame the meaning of words in the curriculum they take for granted, such as "individualism," "progress," "traditions," "ecology," and so forth. Introducing students to the fact that words have a history would seem especially critical in a social-justice-oriented curriculum. Unfortunately, there is no mention of this by the *Handbook's* contributors.

Nor is there a discussion of how to introduce students to the many ways in which the idea of individual intelligence is problematic—for ecological, political, cultural, and moral reasons. Had the contributors read more widely than the writings of their professors and colleagues who share the same silences and historically rooted misconceptions, they might have focused on how to introduce students to the many cultural alternatives that serve as evidence that intelligence is not an attribute of the autonomous individual. That is, social justice teachers might understand how to introduce students to the limited ways they already exercise what can be called ecological intelligence—and to the failure of recognizing that what students too often assume to be their own perceptions are actually based upon the preconceived ideas and value judgments they tacitly learned from their culture. When students ignore the differences which make a difference in their ongoing relationships with other students, parents, and community members—and in their relations with the other participants in the local and global ecological systems of which they are a part—their sense of being an autonomous individual (which was promoted in different ways by René Descartes and by many current educational reformers) cannot help but promote further social and eco-injustices. There are many non-western examples of how the exercise of ecological intelligence fosters mutually supportive community relationships, as well as how to live in more ecologically sustainable ways, but the question to be asked of social justice educators is: How do we help students make the transition to exercising their ecological intelligence in a more conscious way? Somewhere in the 774 pages of the *Handbook* this question should have been raised, particularly since one of the major contributors to the many forms of social injustice that exist in American society is the lack of awareness of how the hyper-subjective sense of individualism and entitlement marginalizes an awareness of how one's actions adversely impact others.

An Ecological Intelligence Approach to Educational Reforms that Address Social Justice Issues

The problem with thinking of social justice in terms of certain groups and categories is that many everyday acts of injustice become too easily ignored. This observation should not be interpreted as saying that the plight of specific groups should be downgraded in importance. Rather, we need to recognize the connections between ideas and behaviors that reinforce the current widespread indifference toward the poverty and limited opportunities of different groups, as well as the everyday acts that exploit, diminish, and in other ways impose limitations on others. These latter manifestations of acting unjustly toward others, when race, class, and gender are not the motivating factors, can be traced to a wide range of destructive attitudes and values. These destructive behaviors range from pure personal greed, the need to dominate others, selfishness, an inability to empathize with others, a diminished self-image, thoughtlessness, and the need to get ahead at all costs, to a growing feeling of powerlessness that leads to striking out at others. Many of these personal attributes are prominent in the promotion of policies that discriminate and exploit identifiable social groups. What is often overlooked is that these are the attributes of individuals who are generally unaware of how their pathological behaviors and ideas are culturally influenced.

The double bind is that for decades classroom teachers and, in particular, professors of education have been reinforcing the belief that students can achieve even greater autonomy if they construct their own knowledge and choose their own values. This has been one of the goals of those promoting critical thinking, and it is now being exploited by the computer industry on the grounds that computer-mediated learning is superior to teacher-directed learning. According to many progressive educators, teacher-directed learning (what has been referred to as "the sage on the stage" and a banking approach to education) is a source of oppression. Universities have further reinforced the idea of individual autonomy by encouraging students to think for themselves, even when they lack the necessary background knowledge and relevant interpretative frameworks. In many instances, the students' acceptance of sitting for hours in classes that have little real interest to them has been achieved by allowing them to choose from a wide array of courses, which again reinforces the value of exercising individual choice in deciding what they want to learn. One of the consequences of this double bind is the growing indifference on the part of many students to the accuracy of information and to the history of ideas. The conceptual inability and unwillingness to question the accuracy and prescriptions of the highly paid demagogues who have established themselves as prominent political leaders can be traced to the failure of classroom teachers and professors to reach an agreement on what students should learn if they are to make informed decisions in a world of competing ideologies, environmental degradation, and growing resistance to cultural colonization.

Bateson's key insights are especially useful for recognizing that addressing social justice issues also requires addressing the cultural assumptions that underlie the myth of individual intelligence. What his insight about the interactive nature of ecosystems, including how cultural ecologies impact natural ecologies that range from the chemical/ genetic level to the climate and ocean systems, brings into focus is that none of us can survive the degradation of the natural systems upon which we depend. Some prominent scientists are now warning that the combination of the loss of habitats and species, overpopulation, and the exploitation of the environment are leading to the sixth extinction of life on this planet. I am not suggesting that this prediction should take top priority over addressing social justice issues, but we do need to take seriously how educational reforms can lead to a reduction in the rate of degradation in the ecologies that are sources of protein and potable water, as well as reducing the degradation that contributes to extreme weather patterns. The current rate of environmental degradation, in combination with the technological revolution that is accelerating changes in the economy as wealth is increasingly being accumulated by those who own the technologies, will have the greatest impact on the already poor and marginalized. Professionals, as well as wage earners, who are in their fifties and older and now without employment as a result of automation and outsourcing, are also swelling the ranks of the newly marginalized and impoverished. The status system that determines who will be the first to be employed may undergo slight revisions, but the ranks of the unemployed and increasingly hopeless will continue to expand beyond the category of groups now identified by educators as the victims of injustice.

Evo Morales, the president of Bolivia, recently reiterated the criticism being made by the leaders of countries being impacted by the climate changes that are affecting glaciers and ocean levels. President Morales has made the case that the cause of the water shortage his country faces is due to the melting of glaciers, and that the melting and disappearance of the glaciers is directly related to the West's system of industrial production and hyper-consumerism. Other examples of environmentally related injustices include the damage to people's health in regions of China, India, and Africa where the toxic wastes of our industrial/consumer lifestyle are being out-sourced. Millions of outmoded computers, cell phones, and other electronic technologies of this cyber era are being outsourced to the poorest communities where hand-labor (often that of children) separates the reusable parts, such as circuit boards, plastics, and metals, from what goes into the local landfills and onto the open fires that release the dioxins and furans which are among the most lethal carcinogens. These recycling efforts enable the poor to escape starvation but leave many children and adults crippled from the lethal toxins released into the air and local water systems.

It takes sustained mental concentration, as well as breaking from the old patterns of thinking, in order to understand Bateson's explanation of how ecosystems, both natural and cultural, undergo changes in response to the multiple forms of information circulating within them. We have been conditioned by our culture's ways of knowing (including its silences) to ignore most of these information exchanges, especially if they don't appear on the surface to have an immediate impact on our well-being or on achieving our immediate goals. Most of us tend not to notice the reduction in the local bird population, but we are likely to be aware of the lack of rainfall—if we are farmers. People who possess a strong sense of their own individuality are less aware of how culture influences both their awareness and the values by which they live. That our embodied experiences are culturally mediated reflects what Bateson refers to as the recursive epistemology of the culture. In short, what the individual takes to be her/his autonomous status, often expressed as the individual's inalienable right to a wide range of freedoms, is actually a result of cultural conditioning to past ways of thinking and experiencing. The argument here is not that all forms of freedom are destructive, even in an environmental sense. Rather, it is that freedom must be exercised in ways that take account of socially just and ecologically sustainable relationships.

Only recently has awareness of injustices surrounding racial and gender relationships led to political action. Unfortunately, it now appears that the growing dominance of market liberal thinking has reduced the awareness of human suffering that led to political protests in the past. The millions of unemployed and the increasing distance between the vast wealth of the few and the millions now falling out of the middle class represent changes that are marginalized by the recursive ideologies of market liberals and libertarians. The challenge of how to respond to Bateson's insight about how information (differences) affects the viability of ecosystems, such as the changes occurring in the economy, is one that educational reformers need to address.

The recent awakening to the prejudicial nature of gender and racial relationships demonstrates that what was previously unrecognized by individuals who assumed they were self-determining is evidence that reforms supported by classroom teachers and professors can filter through and affect changes in different levels of the culture. However, the double bind occurs when classroom teachers and professors share many of the same assumptions and silences that are undermining the traditions of community self-sufficiency. The taken-for-granted assumptions of teachers and professors, as well as their silences, then limit what students will be aware of. This conceptual double bind occurs in other areas of society, especially when the gatekeepers, such as editors, judge twenty-first century thinking in terms of the education they received during the last decades of the twentieth century. In this case, the conceptual double bind limits moving to a new level of understanding. This is also a form of injustice.

Many people still think that the various electronic media—computers, cell phones, etc.—are culturally neutral, and thus can be used either for constructive or destructive purposes. According to this myth, it is the person using the technology who determines how it will be used. As I have explained elsewhere (Bowers, 2000, 2007), this is yet another example of recursive thinking that carries forward the misconceptions of earlier eras when all technological innovations were understood as the expressions of progress. Before explaining how the growing reliance upon electronic media, especially among today's youth, will have an adverse impact on making further gains in addressing social and eco-justice issues, it is necessary to summarize the key features of electronic media—and even the media that now makes face-to-face communication possible.

The following list of the culturally mediating characteristics of computers and other electronic media that are changing the centuries-old patterns of intergenerational renewal of the culture needs to be assessed while keeping Bateson's key insights in mind. It is also important to consider whether what cannot be digitized has a bearing on our ability to recognize and address social and eco-justice issues. In addition, the current use of electronic media by today's youth needs to be kept in mind. According to the research findings of the Kaiser Family Foundation, as reported in the January 20, 2010 issue of the *New York Times*, today's youth between the ages 8 and 18 now spend an average of 47 hours a week using various media ranging from computers, cell phones, iPods, video games, educational videos, to social networking sites. The research study also found that the heaviest users were African-American and Hispanic youth. really?

To reiterate, Bateson's key insights address:

1. The need to be aware of the ways in which earlier patterns of thinking are carried forward and continue to be the taken-for-granted basis of today's thinking;
2. How our future survival depends upon a form of intelligence that is aware of the differences (information) communicated through relationships in both the cultural and natural systems;
3. The importance of using culturally and ecologically informed analogs that ensure that our conceptual maps more accurately take account of the cultural and natural ecologies upon which we are dependent; and
4. The need to make the transition from Level II to Level III learning.

These insights are especially useful for making explicit the different ways in which electronic media, and especially computer-mediated learning, reinforce the western myth of the autonomous individual while at the same time marginalizing the forms of knowledge and embodied experiences that cannot be digitized.

A list of what cannot be digitized is useful for becoming aware of the different ways in which computers reinforce many of the taken-for-granted cultural patterns in the West. It could be further expanded if we were to consider how different languages sustain different "realities," including taken-for-granted behaviors and ways of thinking, awareness of local contexts, spoken narratives, ceremonies, mentoring relationships, and knowledge of the cultural and natural ecosystems. The following list of the culturally mediating characteristics of electronic media technologies needs to be assessed in terms of whether they foster awareness of social justice issues, or whether they further reinforce the acting out of the myth of individual autonomy where awareness of relationships becomes a matter of subjective choice.

1. In spite of the technological advances that make possible the mediated experience of face-to-face communication and a sense of having access to vast quantities of information, what is available to the user of electronic media is largely taken out of context. What cannot be digitized without being fundamentally transformed

includes personal memory, tacit understandings, culturally mediated embodied experiences, mentoring and nurturing relationships,
and the range of psychological and physical sources of repression
and silences that are part of daily life. In short, what electronic
media can communicate is what can be made explicit and digitized—which is only a small part of the knowledge and value
systems that are taken for granted within the world's cultures where
nearly 6000 languages are still spoken. Even within our own culture, the inability of software programmers to recognize, and thus
make explicit, the differences between the culturally diverse intergenerational knowledge and skills that have a smaller ecological
footprint and the forms of knowledge and skills required to sustain
the industrial/consumer-oriented lifestyle means that the current
level of reliance upon computers leads to a huge loss of ecologically
sustainable knowledge.

2. Electronic media, in addition to reinforcing the mistaken idea that
abstract relationships are more real and accessible than face-to-face
relationships, also reinforces the conduit use of language. That is,
the words appearing on the screen, or spoken as part of a video
learning program or game, are seldom recognized as being metaphors whose meanings were framed by the choice of analogs by
earlier thinkers who were reproducing the cultural assumptions of
their era and culture. In short, most uses of electronic media marginalize the awareness that words have a culturally specific history.

3. Because electronic media create the impression that they enable
individuals to escape the spatial and temporal limitations of their
immediate experience, and to explore seemingly endless possibilities, they reinforce the myth of individual autonomy. Public school
and university educators promote the use of computer-mediated
learning on the grounds that computers provide broader and more
accurate access to information, thus enabling students to construct
their own knowledge. Computer-mediated learning may be more
accurate than what is presented in textbooks and by many classroom teachers and professors who fail to inform students when
the knowledge and data being shared with them is based on an
in-depth body of knowledge and when it is only a half-remembered
surface understanding. What is generally overlooked in promoting
a more widespread reliance upon computer-mediated learning is

that classroom teachers and professors are abdicating their responsibility for posing questions and introducing the interpretative
frameworks that enable students to obtain a deeper and more historically informed understanding of the critical issues.

4. Examining educational software programs and the agendas of the
people who write blogs and maintain political action networks
will reveal the recursive cultural assumptions that are seldom made
explicit. Unfortunately, if the classroom teacher and professor take
for granted these same assumptions, which most of their students
are likely to accept, then computer-mediated learning becomes a
powerful colonizing force that undermines the local knowledge
and decision-making that is based on different cultural narratives
and assumptions. Evidence of the increased reliance upon abstract
knowledge, which goes well beyond the educated elites who continue privileging the printed over the spoken word, can be seen in
how even the poorly educated now rely upon a political vocabulary
that fails to take account of the environmental and social justice
issues within their communities.

The many constructive uses of computers, cell phones, etc., have
kept people focused on how the technologies enable them to do what
was not possible before and to ignore the ecologically sustainable intergenerational knowledge and skills that are being marginalized or entirely
lost. The cultural amnesia that accompanies this loss, which includes
both the awareness of traditions that perpetuated discrimination and
exploitation, as well as the traditions that have led to gains in achieving
greater civil liberties and social justice gains, is especially critical now
that the industrial model of production and consumption is exceeding
the self-renewing capacity of natural systems. The cultural amnesia that
is reinforced as computers displace the intergenerational communication
that is often (but not always) the source of the knowledge and skills
essential to maintaining the viability of the local cultural and natural
commons becomes more critical as the market liberal forces are able to
use the new technologies to further automate the workplace, to outsource
jobs, and to exploit the failure of our educational system to introduce
students to an awareness of the cultural and environmental commons.
What the social justice educational reformers do not recognize is that in
a market-dominated economy there needs to be a better balance between

participating in the local cultural commons and dependence upon a money economy. The community gardens and creative arts being promoted in urban areas populated largely by minority and impoverished groups enable youth not only to learn the skills necessary for greater self-sufficiency of their communities but also to discover talents that reduce the need for consumerism.

Electronic media are perceived by many people, particularly in the youth culture, as strengthening relationships. There are few obstructions to communicating with friends, family, colleagues at work, and with people in different parts of the world. These media strengthen the idea that the community that matters is no longer the face-to-face community, but rather, the cyber community. Electronic-mediated communication, as pointed out earlier, allows for only a limited form of information to be shared. The argument here is not that this is unimportant. Rather, the problem is that what people interpret as technological advances in how to share ideas, information, and subjective feelings with others fails to take account of the information that is circulating within the local and global natural systems. Youth and adults who are text messaging, focusing on their computer screens, playing video games, and talking on their cell phones usually are unaware of what is occurring in the surrounding natural environment.

As David Abram points out in *The Spell of the Sensuous* (1996), the sights, smells, and sounds in the local environment we share with other living beings remind us of the interdependent world in which we live. In addition to being sources of aesthetic pleasure and quiet reflection on what is important beyond the values of the marketplace and achieving a higher social status, the messages (differences which make a difference) circulating through the fields, woodlands, rivers, and weather patterns are vitally important if each of us is to assess how to reconcile the quest for greater individual prosperity with our responsibility for the future of both the human and non-human world. The silences where previously there were sounds of birds and nocturnal animals, the appearance of trees budding out weeks ahead of their normal cycle, the change in the number and size of salmon migrating through a river system that has been transformed into the major source of electricity for nearby towns and industrial systems, the disappearance of glaciers, changes in rainfall, and so forth, should be recognized as having life-altering implications. Living in cyber communities desensitizes and thus narrows the awareness of relationships in ways that are critical to our collective survival. To recall Bateson's warning: We cannot survive the destruction of the natural systems that are the source of protein, fiber, potable water, and energy, and that are essential to the full exercise of ecological intelligence. This warning, and the cultural trajectory that it brings into question, are not likely to be understood by the generation of youth who has become addicted to text messaging, cell-phone-based relationships, and knowledge reduction technologies, such as Twitter. Nor is it likely to be understood by people socialized to think of themselves as individuals who make their own decisions—yet continue to think and act in ways that serve the interests of the industrial/consumer culture.

The earlier criticism of educational reformers framing the discussion of social justice issues in ways that reflect late twentieth-century values and economic priorities needs to be taken seriously. Becoming informed about the environmental changes that are already adding to the poverty, dislocation, and poisoning of large numbers of people should be a priority among educational reformers. Developing a theoretical framework for understanding how moving from an individual to an ecological view of intelligence would radically change ideas about educating the already marginalized for jobs that are being outsourced and made redundant by automation. Changes in thinking about social-justice-oriented educational reforms, if informed by an ecological way of thinking, will also shift the focus and narratives from the current emphasis on critical thinking about the different ways in which individuals and social groups are being marginalized to beginning to consider the largely non-monetized intergenerational knowledge, skills, and systems of support that still exist within different ethnic groups, as well as within the mainstream culture.

The questions that need to be asked include: What is the carbon/toxic footprint of these traditions? Do they provide youth the opportunity to discover their talents and interests—and provide for mentoring relationships that strengthen a sense of community? Do they enable students to recognize which traditions carry forward discriminatory and exploitive practices? Do they enable students to recognize the over-arching political/civil liberties frameworks that enable groups rooted in different cultural heritages to respect the idea that other groups share the same civil rights? Do they enable students to recognize the characteristics of modern culture that are based on abstractly grounded cultural assumptions that do not take account of environmental limits? And do they reinforce different cultural approaches to exercising ecological intelligence and thus to being centered more on mutually supportive relationships rather than the pursuit of individual self-interest. Taking these questions seriously will move the discussion of social justice educational reforms beyond what can be achieved by reiterating the old slogans and formulaic thinking of the last decades of the twentieth century.

CHAPTER 4

The Democratic Nature of Ecological Intelligence

The current trends are quite alarming. Religious fundamentalism is on the rise around the world, as is the power of international corporations to influence elections at the international, national, and local levels. The internet and media have enabled extremist groups to gain supporters for their efforts to subvert the democratic process, while youth are increasingly gravitating toward life in cyberspace. None of these trends bodes well for solving the environmental issues related to global warming, the continued contamination of habitats and loss of species, and the other environmental changes that threaten our collective future. These trends are motivated by group and individual self-interest politics. The assumptions underlying their agendas vary widely, but they all share common characteristics, namely, the drive to impose their values and lifestyle on others, and an indifference toward the fate of the future generations who will inherit the natural systems now being degraded by the continued dominance of abstract thinking, greed, unjust wars, and technologies scaled to maximize efficiencies and profits rather than to preserve people's livelihoods and the natural systems. An unwillingness to negotiate, and thus to compromise in the interest of achieving policies that serve the common good for humans and the environment, also is on the ascendancy.

These trends are gravitating toward even greater extremism. The religious fundamentalists want to return to the certainties of earlier centuries, while the market liberals and libertarians justify maximizing profits on centuries-old abstract theories about the self-correcting nature of free markets and how the poverty of individuals cannot be ameliorated by governmental policies. The rapid expansion of ways that people experience being online and thus living in an abstract world of avatars, social networks based on exchanges of personal out-of-context information and gossip, and the quest for constant change pose an equally serious challenge to the future prospects of an informed democracy.

Fortunately, there continue to be sites of resistance to these trends. People in different cultures are working within their communities to strengthen the traditions of mutual support, and to pass on the inter-generational knowledge and skills that reduce dependence upon consumerism. They are also overcoming the psychological scars imposed by western colonization and are actively resisting the forces of economic globalization. The many indigenous cultures that are revitalizing their traditions, as well as the intergenerationally connected face-to-face communities that exist on the margins of the increasingly market-driven regions of the world, are among the hopeful signs that ecological intelligence is being exercised.

The challenge is to clarify two issues of overriding importance. The first is to explain how ecological intelligence is inherently democratic. The second is to explain how to make explicit the recursive misconceptions that underlie the idea of individualism now being promoted around the world. The United States is home to many different expressions of individualism and now exhibits the most pronounced failures in achieving a democratic consensus on environmental and social justice policies. The challenge will be to explain why the current failure in the democratic process cannot be overcome until we move away from the conceptual legacy that has led to our hyper-individualistic culture.

What is needed is an alternative way of understanding democracy —one that is not based on western assumptions about the autonomous individual and the progressive nature of change and that does not reduce the environment to an exploitable resource. Vandana Shiva's principles of Earth Democracy, which use a different vocabulary to restate Bateson's core insights about how our survival depends upon learning to think ecologically, provide an eloquent summary of the democratic relationships and responsibilities that need to become part of our taken-for-granted experience. One of the virtues of her 10 principles is that they do not privilege any one culture's system of knowledge and values over others. At the same time, the 10 principles of Earth Democracy challenge each culture to reflect on the recursive narratives and the other origins of the guiding epistemology that privilege group and individually centered democracy over Earth (or ecological) Democracy.

Vandana Shiva's 10 Principles of Earth Democracy:

1. *All species, peoples, and cultures have intrinsic worth*
   All beings are subjects who have integrity, intelligence, and identity, not objects of ownership, manipulation, exploitation or disposability. No humans have the right to own other species, other people, or the knowledge of other cultures through patents and other intellectual property rights.

2. *The earth community is a democracy of all life*
   We are all members of the earth family, interconnected through the planet's fragile web of life. We all have a duty to live in a manner that protects the earth's ecological processes, and the rights and welfare of all species and all people. No humans have the right to encroach on the ecological space of other species and other people, or to treat them with cruelty and violence.

3. *Diversity in nature and culture must be defended*
   Biological and cultural diversity is an end in itself. Biological diversity is a value and a source of richness, both materially and culturally, that creates conditions of sustainability. Cultural diversity creates the conditions for peace. Defending biological and cultural diversity is the duty of all people.

4. *All beings have a natural right to sustenance*
   All members of the earth community, including all humans, have the right to sustenance—to food and water, to a safe and clean habitat, to security of ecological space. Resources vital to sustenance must stay in the commons. The right to sustenance is a natural right because it is the right to life. These rights are not given by states or corporations, nor can they be extinguished by state or corporate action. No state or corporation has the right to erode or undermine these natural rights or enclose the commons that sustain life.

5. *Earth Democracy is based on living economies and economic democracy*
   Earth Democracy is based on economic democracy. Economic systems in Earth Democracy protect ecosystems and their integrity; they protect people's livelihoods and provide basic needs to all. In the earth economy there are no disposable people or dispensable species or cultures. The earth economy is a living economy. It is based on sustainable, diverse, pluralistic systems that protect nature and people, are chosen by the people, and work for the common good.

6. *Living economies are built on local economics*

Conservation of the earth's resources and creation of sustainable and satisfying livelihoods are most caringly, creatively, efficiently, and equitably achieved at the local level. Localization of economies is a social and ecological imperative. Only goods and services that cannot be produced locally—using local resources and local knowledge—should be produced non-locally and traded long distance. Earth Democracy is based on vibrant local economies, which support national and global economies. In Earth Democracy, the global economy does not destroy and crush local economies, nor does it create disposable people. Living economies recognize the creativity of all humans and create spaces for diverse creativities to reach their full potential. Living economies are diverse and decentralized economies.

Yes!

7. *Earth Democracy is a living democracy*

Living democracy is based on the democracy of all life and the democracy of everyday life. In living democracies people can influence the decisions over the food we eat, the water we drink, and the health care and education we have. Living democracy grows like a tree, from the bottom up. Earth Democracy is based on local democracy, with local communities—organized on principles of inclusion, diversity, and ecological and social responsibility—having the highest authority on decisions related to the environment and natural resources and to the sustenance and livelihoods of people. Authority is delegated to more distant levels of governments on the principle of subsidiarity. Self-rule and self-governance is the foundation of Earth Democracy.

8. *Earth Democracy is based on living cultures*

Living cultures promote peace and create free spaces for the practice of different religions and the adoption of different faiths and identities. Living cultures allow cultural diversity to thrive from the ground of our common humanity and our common rights as members of an earth community.

9. *Living cultures are life nourishing*

Living cultures are based on the dignity of and respect for all life, human and nonhuman, people of all genders and cultures, present and future generations. Living cultures are, therefore, ecological cultures which do not promote life-destroying lifestyles or consumption and production patterns, or the overuse and exploitation of resources. Living cultures are diverse and based on reverence for life. Living cultures recognize the multiplicity of identities based in an identity of place and local community —and a planetary consciousness that connects the individual to the earth and all life.

10. *Earth Democracy globalizes peace, care, and compassion*
Earth Democracy connects people in circles of care, cooperation, and compassion instead of dividing them through competition and conflict, fear and hatred. In the face of a world of greed, inequality, and overconsumption, Earth Democracy globalizes compassion, justice, and sustainability. (Shiva, 2005, pp. 9–11)

Patchouli

If we include the number of indigenous cultures that understand the earth's natural systems as an integral part of their spiritual universe, and that have adapted their cultural practices in ways that are informed by the cycles of renewal within the biotic community, it would not be an over-generalization to claim that many of the world's cultures already live in accordance with most of the principles of Earth Democracy. There are documented instances of abuse and even conflict over territory, but these exceptions do not invalidate the claim that these cultures still adhere to many of the 10 principles. One has only to read such accounts as *Returning to the Teachings* (of the Cree and Ojibway), by Rupert Ross; *Wisdom Sits in Places: Landscape and Language Among the Western Apache*, by Keith Basso; *Priests and Programmers: Technologies of Power in the Engineered Landscape of Bali*, by J. Stephen Lansing; *The Spirit of Regeneration: Andean Culture Confronting Western Notions of Development*, co-edited by Frederique Apffel-Marglin and PRATEC, to recognize that Shiva's 10 principles are not derived from abstract theory. Rather, she derived them from personal observation of many Third World cultures. This is important to recognize, especially for those of us socialized to think in a profoundly different way.

These 10 guiding principles for an ecologically sustainable approach to democracy may seem unattainable to most Americans and Europeans. The fact that other cultures have survived in far less forgiving environments by adhering to most if not all of these principles, while developing complex symbolic traditions and mutual support systems, indicates that making the transition from an individually centered and self-interest democracy to Earth Democracy is a possibility. What will be especially critical is whether we have enough time before the systems upon which we are absolutely dependent begin to collapse. Indeed, as we observe the levels of toxic contamination in the environment, the threat to species in the world's oceans that are a primary source of protein, and the increasing scarcity of potable water—as well as water for agriculture—it should be obvious that we have no choice. Another major reason for introducing changes in our dominant patterns of thinking is that waging war on cultures that do not adopt our values and consumer lifestyle is hugely destructive to the environment. Wars are also destructive of the traditions of intergenerational knowledge that are the basis of the cultural commons, and they divert our own country's resources from addressing poverty and living more ecologically sustainable lives.

I agree!

The challenge will be to recognize the cultural traditions that impede awareness of how our individually centered and self-interest approach to democracy is failing due to its own internal contradictions, and that the pressures are becoming more intense as natural systems become increasingly degraded. The mining of aquifers in the central valley of California, as well as the aquifers underlying regions of the Great Plains, the collapse of the cod fisheries off the Grand Banks, and more recently, the salmon fisheries along the coast of the Pacific Northwest, have disrupted people's taken-for-granted expectation of having a job that will sustain a consumer-dependent lifestyle. The collapse of these and other life-supporting natural systems will force a change in the assumptions that now stand in the way of making the transition to Earth Democracy. The question is whether the reactionary economic, political, and religious forces will promote a civil war or a totalitarian regime—for which significant segments of the American public are already preparing. Given the hold that the ideas and values that gave conceptual direction and moral legitimacy to the industrial/individualistic/consumer-dependent culture have on most Americans' taken-for-granted patterns of thinking, there is only a slim hope that educational reforms will contribute to a peaceful transition to the radically different consciousness required by the practice of Earth Democracy. The recursive cultural patterns upon which most classroom teachers and university professors base their own cutting-edge thinking will be major obstacles to making the needed changes.

Impediments to Making the Transition to Ecological Intelligence and Earth Democracy

Understanding how the ideas of Bateson and Shiva are mutually supportive will help in identifying the patterns of thinking and behaviors that bring into question whether a democratic society based on the politics of self-interest can successfully achieve the reforms needed to slow the rate of environmental degradation. What stands out in Shiva's account of the 10 principles, whether it is the principle that "The earth community is a democracy of all life" or the principle that "Earth Democracy is based on living economies"—or any of the other eight principles—is that the everyday practice of living in accordance with each principle requires giving close attention to relationships. In Bateson's language, attention needs to be given to the differences which make a difference. For example, it requires giving attention to how the use of a technology, such as a pesticide or a new wind turbine, affects the ability of other members of the local ecology to reproduce and thrive. Observing changes in relationships and their impacts should lead to asking whether the conceptual maps—which too often carry forward the misconceptions, prejudices, and silences of earlier times—need to be revised on the basis of what is currently being communicated within and between the different living systems. Observing how butterflies, which are important pollinators, avoid the non-native plants that many home owners associate with beautifying yards, should lead to an awareness that the conceptual map that leads many people to introduce non-native species into rivers and lakes, fields, yards, and so forth, needs to be radically revised. A recent example of human hubris is the introduction of the bighead Asian carp into the Mississippi River Basin, where it has no natural predators. The carp have recently escaped from the aqua farms and are now close to entering Lake Michigan where they will have a devastating impact on the ecology of the Great Lakes. In Bateson's terms, introducing a species that has no natural predators will precipitate a cycle of changes (differences) that will lead to the disappearance of native species of fish—which, in turn, will introduce changes throughout the cultural and natural ecologies.

Bateson's statement that "in no system which shows mental characteristics can any part have unilateral control over the whole. In other words, *the mental characteristics of the system are immanent, not in some part, but in the system as a whole*" (1972, p. 316) goes to the heart of Shiva's way of understanding a democracy among all beings. Again, it is essential to keep in mind that what Bateson refers to as "mental characteristics" is his metaphor for encompassing the various ways in which different forms of life respond to the differences occurring in their environments—ranging from the genetic codes of organisms that dictate the response to changes in chemistry and temperature, to how the inaccurate conceptual maps of humans lead to consequences that go unnoticed within natural systems—until a species goes extinct. Even then, the disappearance of a species may continue to go unnoticed. For Shiva, living systems are sustained by different forms of intelligence that process and respond to the varied information circulating through an ecology. Both Bateson and Shiva agree that the diversity of human cultures and species makes up the unit of survival. Thus, the moral obligation of humans is to carry forward the ecologically sustainable heritage of their culture, as well as to engage in daily practices that do not diminish the prospects of future generations. This requires adapting cultural practices in ways that do not disrupt the flow of the different forms of energy upon which all species depend. As Shiva puts it, "Living cultures are life nourishing," that is, nourishing of the total ecology.

Bateson's warning about the ecological dangers of double bind thinking applies to all 10 of Shiva's principles. A major cause of double bind thinking is the failure to recognize how the vocabulary inherited from the past illuminates and hides, as well as reproduces, the deep cultural assumptions of a human-centered world—including the assumption that the environment only has value when it can be exploited as a commodity. Economic recessions provide an accurate gauge for assessing the core values of a culture. Politicians fear that the democratic process will lead them to being voted out of office if they do not stimulate the economy to exceed past levels of employment and consumption. And indeed, this is likely to happen. The conceptual double bind of recovering the previous levels of consumerism, even when green sources of energy are being utilized, leads to a further decline in the viability of the earth's natural systems. The double bind that continues to be ignored is that the current emphasis on material progress is putting our future at risk. Unfortunately, this unrecognized double bind thinking is based on the assumptions of an earlier era that marginalized awareness of the long-term consequences of a short-term objective.

Other double binds can be seen in students' decisions that are based on the old assumptions (conceptual maps) about how a university degree will enable them to repay their huge student loans even though the work they envision is being outsourced to low-wage regions of the world, as well as being made obsolete by labor-saving technologies. This leads, in turn, to another double bind that goes largely unnoticed; namely, that the vast numbers of unemployed will lack the means to consume what the corporations produce on such a massive scale. These and other conceptual and moral double binds are, in effect, examples of what Bateson refers to as Level II thinking where the culture's recursive patterns of thinking and values are still taken for granted.

The recursive patterns of thinking that are now transforming participatory decision-making, where dialogue, compromise, and negotiation are essential features of a democracy, into polarized ideological camps can be traced to the history of the West. Instead of a willingness to listen carefully and thoughtfully to what is being said by those holding differing ideas and values, political discourse has degenerated into shouting matches, questioning of patriotism, and deliberate misrepresentations that strengthen the slide into friend/enemy thinking.

We need to ask about the origins of the idea that we are autonomous individuals. Can it be traced back to Judaic/Christian theology in which there had to be an accounting for the behavior of individuals in order to determine their destiny in the afterlife? Can it be attributed to the privileging of literacy and abstract/analytical thinking over narratives and face-to-face communication as Eric Havelock, Jack Goody, and Walter Ong have argued? We know that, as a metaphor, the word "individual" has had different meanings in the past. For example, during the feudal era an individual was understood as a "subject" in a hierarchically organized world, while political theorists ranging from John Locke, Jean Jacques Rousseau, and John Stuart Mill argued for new analogs that transform the meaning of the individual into that of a political agent capable of critical thinking and social transformation. Gains in the legal protection of the individual's rights can be traced back to the establishment of habeas corpus in 1215, which was followed by laws and political procedures that further expanded and protected the rights of the individual—including the ownership of physical and intellectual property. The early scientific approach to organizing plants and animals into different classification systems further emphasized the characteristics of individual entities rather than their relationships and roles within ecological communities. Even the introduction of perspective by artists, which in itself frames how relationships are to be understood and appreciated, emphasized the individual as the focal point.

Also contributing to the sense of being an autonomous observer and thinker is the tradition of abstract thinking that underlies differ-

[handwritten margin note: Good point.]

ent philosophic orientations, from Plato's celebrated efforts to explain a social stratification process based on who possessed the rational ability to know the eternal forms, to other rationalists, such as René Descartes, and even empiricists, such as John Locke and David Hume, and now to the many ways of communicating and thinking in today's cyber-culture. Differences in cultural and natural contexts were not taken into consideration, especially after it became accepted that science was based on the "objective" observations of the individual. That is, an individual who is free from cultural influences. This could have been easily seen as a myth if the question were asked about the cultural assumptions that guided the behavior of scientists; namely, their efforts to rationally control the environment, to introduce synthetic chemicals into the environment on the assumption that their discoveries represented progress, and their continuing habit of relying upon a mechanistic vocabulary to describe organic processes.

Perhaps two of the most important influences on the idea of individual autonomy were Adam Smith's *Wealth of Nations* (1776), and later, Herbert Spencer's coining of the phrase "survival of the fittest" to express the dominant ethos during America's early phase of the industrial development that wreaked havoc on the country's natural systems. Smith's nearly half-million-word tome has not been read by the millions of Americans who have accepted popularized reinterpretations of the economic and political implications of laissez faire—which has been given special legitimacy by the Nobel Prize-winning economist Milton Friedman. The idea that market forces should be free of government regulation, that individuals should be unrestrained in their pursuit of wealth, that there is an "invisible hand" (mentioned only once in Smith's writings), and that competition not only benefits all levels of society but also separates the deserving from the weak and indifferent, reflects more than a hint of Spencer's Social Darwinism that is now back in vogue under a slightly different vocabulary.

In effect, these abstract ideas—that is, where local markets that exhibit the values and constraints of the local cultures in which they are embedded were dismissed in favor of a supposedly natural law that governs economic relationships in all cultures—strengthened the myth of individual autonomy in a number of ways. The two most important made the individual pursuit of wealth a primary goal in life and strengthened the idea that self-interest is the primary source of motivation in a world of unrelenting competition. Although Adam Smith's early reputation was established with the publication of the *Theory of Moral Sentiments* (1759), in which he argued that face-to-face relationships within communities would reduce the desire to economically exploit others, his misinterpreted legacy has become the cornerstone of the idea that free markets and the individual pursuit of wealth should be the primary goals in life.

Academics, while being critical of how free market policies have consigned millions to lives of unrelenting poverty and allowing a minority to obtain both wealth and political power, also rely upon the rules that govern what Alvin Gouldner refers to as the "culture of critical discourse" (1979, p. 28). Chief among these rules is the need to achieve progress through a competitive process of argumentation, exhibiting a more elaborated speech code than those who hold differing ideas, and the ability to present "objective" evidence. The rules governing those who are allowed to participate in the culture of critical discourse are understood to have the same universal standing as the principal of free markets. It is also important to note that the oral traditions of different cultures are excluded from what constitutes legitimate speech and evidence—which rely upon both abstract theories and data.

Another source of influence on the myth that individuals are autonomous thinkers and actors includes the conduit view of language that is reinforced in public schools, universities, and in everyday communication in homes, churches, entertainment venues, and so forth. This view of language, as Michael Reddy (1979) has pointed out, reinforces the mistaken idea that words convey ideas that originate within the individual's thought process. What is overlooked, as I have written about elsewhere (2008, 2009, 2010), is that words have a history and reproduce in the present the analogs settled upon by earlier thinkers, as well as the deep cultural assumptions of their era. According to Bateson, the vocabulary (which is the basis of the conceptual "maps") carries forward, over hundreds of years, the recursive patterns of thinking of the culture— which individuals ignore when assuming that their ideas and value judgments are the outcome of their original thinking.

These recursive linguistic patterns are being strengthened further in public schools where the professional education of teachers is guided by different interpretations of the progressive ideology that, ironically, are shared by the proponents of the industrial culture that is awakening to the profitability of new, energy-saving technologies. The centerpiece of the indoctrination that is a core feature of teacher education programs is that pedagogy and the curriculum should help students to construct their own ideas and choose their own values. As will be explained in later chapters, the emphasis on computer-mediated learning is also thought to strengthen the students' ability to construct their own interpretations of events, to choose what are appropriate behaviors—and even to rewrite the endings of traditional stories in ways that fit more with their own interests and values.

A dominant characteristic of today's political discourse is the cultural amnesia that is so widely shared. The modern, progressive ethos reinforces the idea that traditions are irrelevant, if not obstructions, to participating more fully in the emergent cyber-culture that allows for greater expression of personal freedom and instant gratification. If this ethos is correct, and if the assumption is valid that all the knowledge and techniques that individuals will need are now available on the internet, and if their innate propensity is to construct their own knowledge, then the condition of cultural amnesia would not be considered as a social and political pathology—but as a liberating force. Ignorance of the past will also be seen as liberating individuals from any sense of guilt about not taking responsibility for the loss of important gains made in the past, such as gains in the areas of civil liberties and social justice movements.

The politics of group and individual self-interest have now become so polarized that many groups reject all legislative proposals that do not benefit them directly. The tradition of political decision-making that focuses on the common good promoted by civic-oriented individualism has largely, though not entirely, disappeared. Ironically, the convergence of the market liberal and libertarian ideologies with the so-called progressive and emancipatory trend that has dominated colleges of education over the last 50 or so years has contributed to the nihilism that now characterizes group and self-interest politics.

This claim will be rejected by the progressive and emancipatory educators who are vociferous critics of the social injustices they view as inherent in the political and economic agenda of the market liberals and libertarians. Their criticisms, however, fail to take account of the assumptions they share with them. These assumptions include thinking of change as inherently progressive, that this is a human-centered world, that individuals should strive for greater autonomy, and that these assumptions should be universally shared. These assumptions also share many of the same silences, such as a lack of awareness of the recursive conceptual patterns they take for granted, the map/territory problem that leads to double bind thinking, and a lack of awareness of the ecological importance of the cultural and environmental commons. The market liberals promote educational reforms that prepare students for the workplace while at the same time saturating the students' environments, and thus their consciousness, with commercials and consumer items tailored to ever-changing youth fashions and cyber-technologies.

The continual transformation by market forces of what remains of the cultural commons further socializes youth to think that all aspects of daily life involve consumer relationships and dependencies. As Kirkpatrick Sale points out in *Rebels Against the Future: The Luddites and Their War on the Industrial Revolution* (1995), the industrial approach to production and consumption requires an autonomous individual who lacks the intergenerational knowledge and skills, and thus is dependent upon consumerism, to meet daily needs. Creating a state of consciousness where freedom, progress, and individual autonomy become interchangeable goals in life requires the alienation of the individual from the traditions of community. Encouraging students to construct their own knowledge and to "rename the world of the previous generations," as Paulo Freire puts it in *Pedagogy of the Oppressed* (1971, p. 76), contributes to self-interest politics. If there is nothing in the individual's culture that is worth renewing and passing on to future generations, then political decisions can be based on the immediate interests of the individual. Both John Dewey and Freire view all cultural traditions as obstructions to individual freedom and social progress. One of the pedagogical implications of their views is that teachers are not to engage students in the study of the traditions that are the basis of the students' diverse cultural backgrounds, as this represents what Freire calls the banking approach to education. For Dewey, cultural traditions become important only as the focus of what needs to be reconstructed through the experimental approach to problem solving—which he considers the only valid approach to knowledge, and thus should be adopted by all cultures. Today's teacher educators are less likely to quote Dewey and Freire. Instead, they find sufficient justification for promoting individually centered "constructivist learning" in the romantic belief that the students' essential nature is in their creative approach to organizing their own freedom.

What is especially important is that the promotion of individual autonomy by market liberal/libertarians, as well as by progressive/emancipatory educators, excludes any consideration of the warnings by environmentalists that humans would need an additional planet to support the West's current level of consumption if it were adopted by all the people in the world. Market liberals (but not the libertarians) have recently discovered that by adopting the language of sustainability they can further expand their markets and thus increase their profits. Only a small minority of progressive/emancipatory educational reformers are beginning to recognize that there is an ecological crisis, but they have not engaged in the reflexive Level III learning advocated by Gregory Bateson and Vandana Shiva.

Today's followers of Dewey and Freire are caught in what can be called the reified paradigm they acquired from their professors who promoted the late twentieth-century legacy of liberalism that did not take account of environmental limits. Unfortunately, the recursive patterns of thinking underlying their socialization continue to perpetuate the reductionist view of traditions established by the Enlightenment thinkers. The conceptual maps borrowed from these earlier thinkers still prevent these progressive/emancipatory educational reformers from recognizing the intergenerational knowledge and skills, which are today's living traditions, being carried forward in every community. That many of these traditions represent alternatives to being dependent upon jobs that are disappearing, and to the crushing debt of consumerism that is forcing people out of their houses, has not led to a revision in thinking about ecological and community-sustaining traditions. Recognizing that some traditions are the best defense against the ideological and technological forces leading to a police state, and the best answer we have for limiting the spread of capitalism and the environmental destruction that it promotes in the name of progress, may lead to revising the analogs that inform the progressive-oriented language and thought patterns.

Why the Transition to Exercising Ecological Intelligence May Be the Best (perhaps only) Hope for Restoring a Democratic Society

The tragedy of the cultural commons is far more complex than what Garrett Hardin represents as the tragedy of the environmental commons. Easily grasped is his famous yet hypothetical example of how the self-interest of the farmer who gains by adding more cattle to a shared pasture has the effect of placing a future burden on the land's other users as the pasture becomes over grazed. The same tragedy is being repeated in other areas of the environmental commons by corporations and individual property owners who are focused on maximizing profits—which range from corporations mining coal, aquifers, and fisheries, to the cutting of old-growth forests. The underlying combination of cultural assumptions is mutually supportive and simply referred to by the general public as "progress." Unfortunately, this form of progress trumps the common good.

The tragedy of the cultural commons is far more complex than the enclosure of the environmental commons—because it is far difficult to recognize. But the result is equally ruinous for both the human and non-human communities. The intergenerational knowledge, skills, and mutually supportive relationships that lead to the preparation of food according to a traditional recipe, to the performance of a group of musicians, to various expressions of skill and knowledge of a craft, to acts of resistance to threats to traditional civil liberties, are carried on in every community. What is important about these activities is that what is being intergenerationally passed along and renewed cannot be as easily privatized and monetized as has been the case with the selling off of the natural commons. When the intergenerational knowledge and skills are monetized, they cease to be part of the commons. Furthermore, the largely symbolic nature of the cultural commons, unless it takes the form of prejudicial and hate-driven practices, is oriented toward passing on what enables people to live less monetized lives. In most instances, relationships connected through cultural commons activities are not motivated by self-interest and individual competition but, rather, by cooperation and the desire to share. Too often, these values are perverted by the psychological factors that come into play because of the socialization process in a culture where contradictory values and pressures make it necessary for the individual's sense of self-worth and respect to be earned. The important point is that in the mainstream culture most people have been socialized to equate personal self-worth and success with the acquisition of material wealth. This conceptual orientation leads most Americans to ignore the importance of finding meaning and a sense of identity in the cultural commons.

Especially important is the need to clarify the many ways in which the positive, life-supporting, and enhancing aspects of the local cultural

commons are being enclosed—and how this process is critical to undermining the democratic decision-making that makes the common good a
priority over the politics of group and individual self-interest. One of the
fundamental differences between the cultural and environmental commons is that privatizing and turning the environmental commons into
products that can be sold can be calculated as adding to the rate of economic growth. The enclosing of some aspect of the cultural commons,
such as addicting youth to industrial foods which then leads them to
ignoring their home and ethnic traditions of food, also adds to what can
be measured as growth in corporate profits. The aspects of the cultural
commons that have not yet been turned into new exploitable markets
are part of the taken-for-granted experience that is not measurable in
economic terms.

If we were to do an ethnographic study of how people participate
in the cultural commons—growing a garden, preparing a meal, playing an instrument, talking with neighbors, writing a family biography,
doing pro bono work that protects the rights of immigrants, and so
forth—it would be possible to compare the carbon and toxic footprint
of the person involved in these activities with the footprint of the person
who has fully embraced the lifestyle and ideology of the autonomous
individual who is dependent upon consumerism to meet both physical
and emotional needs. A conversation with a neighbor, working at a
pottery wheel, playing a game of chess, engaging in various kinds of
volunteerism, bending metal over a white-hot forge, and so forth, involve a
duration of time and embodied experiences that are profoundly different from the experience of time characterized by not knowing what to
do except driving to the shopping mall or watching the thousands of
commercials on T.V. In addition to the difference in the carbon and
toxic footprints between cultural commons and consumer-oriented
experiences, there is also a difference in the health and happiness associated with the two lifestyles—which can be easily documented.

If we were to give close attention to the different activities, as
well as the interpersonal and interspecies relationships that are part of
cultural commons experiences, it would become evident that they require
exercising more of the characteristics of ecological intelligence. Unlike
the culturally mediated embodied experiences of being a consumer or
interacting with a technology, such as a cell phone, computer, or video
game—which primarily amplify the sense of being an autonomous

individual who relies upon vision and instrumental reasoning—cultural commons experiences require giving more attention to relationships and to the differences which make a difference within those relationships. Attention to the differences becomes important in determining how to achieve certain desired results, which may vary from being aware of whether the temperature of a kiln is right for the type of glaze that is used, to whether an additional spice needs to be added to a curry dish, to whether the growing season has reached the point where certain reeds will have the right color for a piece of weaving. Whether playing a game or working the soil for planting, all the senses are involved in a way that differs from watching television, driving a car, or walking through a shopping mall—which are visually oriented experiences. Walking though an open field, along a beach, or through a forest involves a complex sensory connection with the multiple ecosystems that become part of a culturally mediated embodied experience. These experiences may prompt Level III thinking about the educational process that reinforces the assumptions that are part of the heritage of western abstract thinkers, and possibly an increased awareness that the consumer-driven lifestyle is threatening the prospects of future generations to become aware that they are participants in the democracy of all living ecosystems.

There are other aspects of the cultural and environmental commons that are not adequately understood, especially in light of how public schools and universities reinforce students in thinking of themselves as autonomous individuals—which too often translates into thinking of democracy as voting one's self-interests. Increasingly, the way self-interest is understood is being shaped by changes in an economy, such as the automation of the workplace which enables employers to reduce the need for workers and to escape from paying health benefits, and the outsourcing of production to low-wage regions of the world. Thus, so-called democratic decision-making is increasingly becoming a matter of voting one's self economic interests. And, with the market liberal majority of the U.S. Supreme Court voting that the political donations of corporations are the expression of free speech guaranteed by the Constitution, democracy as practiced in the United States is more and more dominated by the pursuit of economic advantage over others—including the natural systems that will lose the protection earlier generations of environmentalists were able to enact into law. With corporations now being fully enfranchised with the same rights as individuals, and with public schools and universities relying upon a variety of strategies for promoting the idea of individual autonomy and reliance upon purposive rationality as the source of individual empowerment, the prospects of returning to the civil ideals of the Founding Fathers are fading fast. The slippery political slope these developments have put the country on raises questions about how to achieve the change in consciousness required to make the turn away from the fascist future supported by the growing alliance of corporations, the military establishment, and the millions of Americans who support the use of torture and police-state technologies, and who view the Joseph Goebbels-style media demagogues as sources of political wisdom.

As the exercise of ecological intelligence relies on all the senses for knowledge of the changes constantly occurring in the local cultural and environmental commons, it involves making informed decisions that take account of the patterns that connect—including how decisions will affect the behavior of other participants in the local cultural and natural ecosystems. One of the key points that Shiva makes in her 10 principles of Earth Democracy is that democracy involves reciprocal responsibilities in all relationships—including those involving the non-human community. Her insight echoes Bateson's statement that no part of the system can have unilateral control over the whole—that is, humans cannot exercise democratic decision-making that excludes the life-renewing capacity of the other participants in the larger ecological systems. (Before the reader jumps all over Bateson for seeming to make a statement about the equal worth of all beings, it needs to be kept in mind that he also recognizes what he refers to as an ecology of weeds and of bad ideas.) What is overlooked in the current way of thinking and practicing democratic decision-making is that it has increasingly been reduced to voting for special issues and for candidates who represent what is supposed to be a consensus way of thinking. The scope of democratic decision-making is further limited by the fact that the elected representatives who are to negotiate with other supposed representatives of the people usually do so far from the daily lives of their constituents. That the political process requires being constantly in search of donations in order to win the next election further compromises the democratic process. In effect, the so-called democratic system is flawed in a number of ways that ensure that democracy is becoming degraded to the point where the common good, as understood by Bateson and Shiva, is seldom considered.

Democracy is practiced on a daily basis in the relationships and activities carried on within the cultural commons—and in the natural commons. That is, in participating in activities involving others, whether playing a game, participating in cultivating a community garden, or helping someone make repairs on her/his house, there is a constant stream of differences which make a difference—in the expression and tone of voice of the Other, in how certain chemicals react to the introduction of other chemicals, in the reaction of animals to non-native plants, and so forth. These differences, to recall Bateson's point, are the information circulating through the system, and the person who gives attention to the complexity of this information and adjusts her/his responses accordingly is exercising ecological intelligence. If the responses to these differences are not ignored because of pre-conceived ideas about what the outcome should be, such as turning some aspect of the commons into a commodity, or ignored because of prior socialization that reinforces the idea that the individual is the only intelligent participant and thus not needing to learn from what the other participants in the ecology are communicating, then the exercise of ecological intelligence is also the practice of local democracy. Of course there are abuses, and there are people who reduce democracy to slogans while engaging in authoritarian relationships—even in situations involving mentoring. And there are also educational and social justice reformers who cloak their real agenda of cultural imperialism behind the god-words of democracy and emancipation.

There are two ways of understanding democracy. As an activity, democracy is an integral part of the largely non-monetized sharing of intergenerational knowledge and skills that sustain a wide range of activities that are largely taken for granted. The more traditional view of democracy is as a decision-making process that occurs on a specific date, related to deciding specific issues, carried out by distant representatives constantly tempted to accept large donations, and increasingly mediated by technologies that further reduce the need to exchange ideas on a face-to-face basis with people who hold alternative values and points of view. This latter view of democracy can be seen in the following description of the issues considered at a recent university conference titled "What is Democracy? Democracy and Space: Critical Dimensions" held in the Northwest.

The policy issues addressed included the following:

Modern liberal democracy can be seen in terms of formal contracts, abstract rights, and bureaucratic institutions, but addressing the concrete reality of contemporary democracies arguably requires making the question of space central. How is democracy configured as a national territory and how does that territory define, exclude, and condition its citizens? How are democratic cities planned, who controls public space, and what kinds of collective action are deemed legitimate in urban space? To what degree can we say liberal democracies actually operate according to principles of inclusion in the face of such phenomena as residential segregation, unequal distribution of public funding, and the operation of penal systems?

Framing democratic issues in terms of political spatial boundaries, as well as the issues to be debated by politicians and academics, may lead to interesting papers and discussions. Unfortunately, the assumptions underlying this way of thinking about democracy are the same ones that ensure the failure to understand its daily role in renewing the cultural commons and resisting their enclosure by market forces. These assumptions include thinking of democracy as individuals expressing their views on policy issues—particularly policy issues related to social justice and the organization and uses of public spaces. Yes, these issues are important. However, when framed in this way, the micro, face-to-face dimensions of democracy are ignored, which, in turn, leads to ignoring the essential democratic nature of ecological intelligence. What Bateson describes as the information being exchanged in all ecosystems, ranging from the micro-chemical/genetic level, to how cultural practices impact habitats and species, to changes caused by global warming—which is summed up in his phrase a "difference which makes a difference"—confronts humans with a political choice in how to respond to the differences (information coded in many different ways) being communicated by changes in the environment.

In order to understand how Bateson's key insights can be understood as having profound political implications, it is necessary to consider Michel Foucault's way of understanding the exercise of power—and how the exercise of power can lead to democratic relationships, and when it becomes authoritarian. In *Michel Foucault: Beyond Structuralism and Hermeneutics* (1982), by Hubert L. Dreyfus and Paul Rabinow, Foucault writes the Afterword titled "The Subject and Power." This essay is arguably his most insightful statement on the nature of power. His understanding of the micro-expression of power supports what Bateson refers to as differences which lead to responses that lead, in turn, to an expanding cycle of differences. For Foucault, power is expressed as "an action upon the actions of Others" (p. 221). He goes on to explain how different regimes of truth—religious, ideological, scientific, etc.— dictate the different ways in which power is exercised and the ends which are achieved. If Bateson's arguments about the recursive epistemological structures, map/territory distinctions, double bind thinking and acting, and the difference between Level II and Level III thinking are compared to Foucault's way of understanding the cultural influences on the exercise of power, it would be clear that their two theories complement and bring out the importance of what is understated in each other's theory. Bateson's understanding of an ecology, including the nature of ecological intelligence, does not make explicit that responding to the differences which make a difference involves an action upon an action—that is, the exercise of power. Nor does he make explicit that responding to differences is political in the sense of affecting the behavior, and thus life-altering chances, of other participants in the cultural and natural ecologies. He continually warns against humans thinking that they can control the environment and that they are the only source of intelligence. And Foucault, who understands power as being expressed in every relationship (which he understands as an action upon the action of the Other), is explaining the ecology of power without specifically referring to it as an ecology.

The exercise of ecological intelligence leads to an action upon an action that can take at least three forms of expression. That is, the form that the action or response takes may be consciously supportive, an expression of indifference, or actively in opposition. The response may also lead to questions, to attempts to model and make suggestions for improvement, and may mentor others in carrying out the task in non-environmentally destructive ways. These behaviors are expressions of power, and in the vocabulary of democratic discourse they represent a "vote" for what is seen as acceptable and in need of support, as well as what needs to be opposed. Even a lack of awareness and concern are expressions of the individual's political preferences. The action upon an action (or difference, in Bateson's language) is the culturally mediated embodied exercise of democracy. The awareness of information being communicated through the relationships within natural systems also leads to the exercise of power—that is, a response (an action) to what is being communicated by the Other. This also involves a political relationship. When the relationship is nourishing rather than exploitative (that is, where capitalism and an anthropocentric way of thinking are the regimes of truth) it then fits more closely with Shiva's principles of Earth Democracy.

It is widely understood that the western approach to democracy places an emphasis on the legal right of individuals to express their ideas about how issues of the community and state should be settled, and on the importance of majority rule. This interpretation of democracy reflects the assumptions and silences of the political theorists who made the argument that individuals should be free to express their views on the form of government they want, and on the rules and regulations that everybody is to follow. Previous and current experiences of oppression and the denial of basic human rights led to this more legalistic understanding of democracy. Unfortunately, these early political theorists ignored that all human-with-human, and human-with-nature, interactions are expressions of preferences and power and thus are political. The actions upon the actions of Others, that Foucault describes as the exercise of power, too often ignore a fatal shortcoming that is magnified when democracy is elevated to that of an explicit political code that legitimates voting behaviors. As an explicit governing political code, the emphasis on the rights of individuals fails to take account of whether the voters are informed about the issues upon which they are voting. It also fails to take account of whether the voters possess authoritarian personalities and equate the common good with what serves their self-interest. There are similar problems in how individuals respond to changes in their relationships with others and to what is being communicated by changes occurring in the surrounding natural systems. Voting one's political preferences may not involve taking responsibility for responses that are destructive and based on ignorance and preconceived patterns of thinking. If society is to begin making the transition to valuing and nourishing ecological intelligence, rather than continuing to reinforce the recursive ideal of individual autonomy and context-free thinking, it will be necessary to learn how to give more attention to relationships and to the consequences of behaviors that ripple through the surrounding cultural and natural ecosystems.

What is often overlooked is that the democratic process has often led to autocratic systems of government. The potential for failure can be seen when considering how the fascist regimes that came into power between the two world wars were the outcome of democratic elections. Now, in the United States, the democratic process that takes place in presidential and congressional elections involves a large percentage of votes being cast for politicians who support the expansion of the American empire, who want to restrict women's biological rights, who support corporate welfare, who deny that there is an ecological crisis, and who think that corporate greed is in the public interest. The ways in which public schools and universities reinforce individuals to think for themselves regardless of their depth of relevant knowledge, and to assume that their ideas and knowledge are always beyond questioning, help ensure that democratic decisions will continue to support wars of aggression. If it is suggested that these self-proclaimed autonomous individuals are not adequately informed and are less autonomous than they want to believe, they will claim that their right to individual self-expression is being threatened. We are collectively caught in a double bind that has its roots in the abstract thinking of the philosophers and social theorists who identified the limited set of analogs that led to thinking of individuals as autonomous and self-creating.

Not only does the exercise of ecological intelligence lead to a heightened awareness of the difference between sustainable and non-sustainable relationships in the cultural and natural ecologies, but it also has a special role to play in resisting the enclosure of the cultural commons by individuals and corporations who vote their short-term economic interests. Unlike individuals who are Level II thinkers, and who also assume that they are autonomous thinkers, those who exercise ecological intelligence not only require Level III thinking but also the ability to continually revise ideas and values in light of the new information that comes from an awareness of changes in the interacting cultural and natural ecosystems. Being informed about how to be a supportive participant in the relationships Shiva describes as the Earth Democracy —which are both local and global—is just one the responsibilities of exercising ecological intelligence.

If we exclude the worst social injustices of the cultural commons of some communities, and focus instead on the traditions of intergenerational knowledge and skills that reduce dependence upon consumerism and have a low carbon and toxic footprint, then it is possible to recognize the community-centered relationships and activities where democratic decision-making is becoming more critical. Ecological intelligence is used in mentoring relationships, in carrying on and in refining the different traditions that have been intergenerationally passed along—in working with wood, in the creative arts, in gardening, in turning local resources into products that can be exchanged or used as part of a local currency system. To repeat: Ecological intelligence involves adjusting what has been learned from previous relationships in the different cultural and natural ecologies in ways that do not lead to actions that adversely impact the lives of other participants—whether human or non-human. It also involves Level III thinking that makes explicit the recursive patterns of thinking and language usage that are otherwise taken for granted. People who exercise ecological intelligence reinforce other members of the community, especially those who are consciously engaged in cultural commons activities; but they are a minority both in terms of numbers and in terms of what represents the dominant ideological orientation in the country.

The critical point is that what remains of the cultural commons is being viewed by self-interest individuals and corporations as activities and relationships to be exploited and brought into the system of industrial production and consumption. At the beginning of the Industrial Revolution, when the environmental commons were fenced off so that the land could be used to meet the demands of the emerging industrial culture, this process of turning what was shared in common into what became privatized and monetized was known as "enclosure." This word also applies to monetizing the cultural commons and to turning them into products to be sold. Indeed, there are few aspects of the cultural commons that the industrial system of production and consumption are morally prohibited from turning into money-making activities. Even the thought patterns of the human brain are being studied in order to sell drugs that will erase unwanted memories—which will serve the interests of governments as well as the pharmaceutical industries. While this tradition of economic enclosure is now strengthened by a variety of cultural forces, ranging from Social Darwinism to the current hyper-sense of individual autonomy in a competitive world where money is the dominant value, there are other forms of enclosure that are threatening one of the main alternatives we have to reducing the ecological footprint of humans. Enclosure also occurs when classroom teachers and university professors fail to engage students in the study of the nature of the local cultural commons and the historical forces of enclosure. Most students lack the vocabulary for making explicit and naming the largely non-monetized traditions that are part of their daily lives. Ironically, when cultural commons activities are enclosed and transformed into consumer products, most students, like their parents, are likely to equate their increased dependency upon the increasingly unpredictable money economy with progress. This lack of awareness, along with the tradition of associating participation in a money economy with being an autonomous individual, is just one aspect of the cultural amnesia that is fostered by the increased reliance upon electronic-based thinking and communication (which will be examined more closely in the next chapter).

People who are engaged in the local cultural commons—participants in non-industrial approaches to food, creative arts, crafts, etc.—are conscious stewards of the intergenerational traditions they are carrying forward and adapting to today's circumstances. That is, they are aware of the forces of enclosure, which is not the case of most people who were indoctrinated by public schools and universities to play by the rules governing success in the industrial/consumer culture. Today's youth, who spend many hours each day engaged in electronic social networking, are even less aware of the different forms of enclosure occurring in the local and global cultural commons. The transformation of skills and mutual support systems that contribute to less environmentally destructive lives into yet new areas of consumer dependency is a difference which makes a difference. Students should be educated to recognize and respond politically to the cultural forces that are increasing their dependency upon economic and political forces over which they have no control.

As intergenerational knowledge and skills are turned into new products, or marginalized by the constant stream of new electronic technologies, students need to be able to recognize that the protection of the community's traditions of ecologically sustainable and mutually supportive relationships is the political arena in which they should become engaged. Elected representatives, located in distant sites where economic pressures are so intense that the voices of their local communities cease to be heard, are part of what is now the dysfunctional legacy of a political process based on the idea that the pursuit of self-interest contributes to the common good. Politics that are responsive to ecological intelligence require both a greater effort on the part of educators to foster greater awareness of the differences occurring in the natural and cultural systems, and the ability of youth to decide whether these life-supporting or life-threatening differences should be supported or challenged. The differences which make a difference represent the local contexts in which democratic decisions need to be made.

CHAPTER 5

How Ecological Intelligence Leads to Reframing the Origins of Moral Values

Several of Bateson's key ideas help to clarify a recursive epistemic pattern that is at the root of the idea that individuals make autonomous decisions in the area of moral values—and that the more autonomous individuals become the more their exercise of individual intelligence puts moral values on an individually determined rational basis. As the educational goal of promoting greater individual autonomy has a long history in the West and has not included an awareness of the moral implications of how to live within environmental limits, it is necessary to consider the characteristics of ecological intelligence as an alternative to the recursive patterns and double bind thinking that underlie this goal. The irony is that the education section of UNESCO is now promoting reforms in teacher education that foster the students' own construction of knowledge and critical thinking—which supposedly will contribute to an ecologically sustainable future. There could be no better example of double bind thinking or better example of how the misconceptions of the past continue to be perpetuated in the name of progress.

Understanding the characteristics of ecological intelligence can be derived partly from an auto-ethnography of our own culturally mediated embodied experiences, partly from the insights of Gregory Bateson, and partly from the study of indigenous cultures. For example, the survival of the Quechua of the Peruvian Andes depends upon a conceptual/moral framework that promotes observing and responding to the differences which make a difference in weather patterns, soil conditions, changes in behavior of animals, and so forth. The natural world, which they carefully observe, is viewed as nurturing them and thus is not to be exploited. In short, the effort to identify the characteristics of ecological intelligence, which vary from culture to culture, should not be interpreted as an ideal, rationally based philosophical argument. Rather, the connections between a culture's practice of ecological intelligence and its moral values, or the lack of a connection, can be empirically observed if we are able to set aside the recursive conceptual patterns that are not recognized because of their being taken for granted. Throughout the following discussion, an emphasis will be placed on what can be called the linguistic colonization of the present by the past—that is, how we remain under the influence of historical forces that current misconceptions continue to hide.

One of the more powerful forces of recursive thinking has its origins in the myth that humans have a God-given right to exploit the natural environment, which can be found in a literal interpretation of the *Book of Genesis*. Surely, it must have had antecedents in the oral traditions of the region in which it originated. However, the mythopoetic narrative that was committed to print, and that described the process of God's creation, has had a powerful influence on the millions of Christians who have interpreted it as giving them permission to exploit the natural environment. While much of the Biblical narrative is metaphorical, and thus open to a wide range of interpretations, the passage that has been taken literally reads: "And God blessed them, and God said to them, Be fruitful, and multiply, and replenish the earth, and subdue it: and have dominion over the fish of the sea, and over the fowl of the air, and over every living thing that moveth upon the earth." (Genesis, I, 28) While the influence of this Biblical passage is most prominent in America, even western cultures that have taken a more secular turn have retained this anthropocentric view of human/nature relationships—which is being challenged only by the small sector of society that is beginning to exercise ecological intelligence.

The entire responsibility for the current level of pillaging what remains of the earth's life-sustaining natural bounty, however, should not be entirely placed on the passage from the *Book of Genesis*. Other assumptions became part of the collective narratives that have led to today's dominant way of valuing the environment as an exploitable resource. While some Christians are now beginning to think in terms of stewardship, rather than in terms of subduing and dominating nature, the *Genesis* passage is the focus of Bateson's criticism (cited earlier) of the continued inability of humans to recognize that they are integral participants in the multi-layered and interdependent ecological systems that range from the symbolic foundations of culture to the genetic/chemical levels of existence.

Recognizing that human survival is dependent upon the capacity to adapt to the information being communicated within the world's cultural and natural ecosystems is essential to making the transition to exercising ecological intelligence. As humans begin to make this transition, their approach to moral values will undergo a transition similar to how ecological intelligence reframes democratic practices. But it is first necessary to understand the many ways in which the recursive conceptual patterns that people take to be real, and thus "normal," are bringing us to the edge of a life-ending ecological catastrophe. The most obvious yet most daunting and reactionary forces that reinforce the idea that the individual is an autonomous moral agent are seen in the many ways that children, youth, and adults are told to make their own decisions—albeit with an increasingly surface understanding of national and world events. The use of personal pronouns constantly establish the individual as an autonomous moral agent—even when the contingencies of reinforcement and punishments are clearly visible. There are social rewards for being a consumer, for conforming to group expectations, for embracing the hyper-patriotism of the demagogues and corporations, for following the rules laid down by parents, teachers, and professors. Ultimately, it is still assumed that individual intelligence is the source of the moral decision to conform to the value system of others. The social systems in which individuals find themselves may make unrealistic demands that can only be met by some form of cheating, yet efforts to avoid failure made inevitable by these systems are regarded as the moral missteps of the individual. Most of everyday life, however, involves making moral decisions that are the result of societal pressures that go unacknowledged because of the need to maintain the illusion of moral autonomy.

Included among the many fads that sweep through the field of teacher education are the various expressions of progressive education— from the child-centered reforms of the early 1920s, to today's emphasis on encouraging students to construct their own knowledge, choose their own values, and choose even the careers they want to follow. Over the years this has been a very powerful form of indoctrination. It is still assumed that the students will discover how their own moral values relate to the important social and environmental issues of the day. This rarely happens as so much of the student's world is taken for granted, and thus beyond questioning. What students learn in classrooms where the teacher, to use a popular phrase of this movement, is a guide on the side and not a sage on the stage, is that they are free to be authentic—which really means free to make moral choices within the conceptual confines established by cultural forces that are seldom made explicit. Even the self-proclaimed radical educational reformers who make emancipation from oppressive social norms their primary agenda assume that fostering the students' ability to subject all aspects of the adult world to critical inquiry leads to a more just and free society. The irony is that these promoters of critical inquiry as the educational alternative to the socialization process that occurs as part of the languaging/reality sustaining processes of everyday life fail to recognize the deep cultural assumptions they share with the industrial culture they constantly criticize. Critical inquiry is still assumed to be the engine of progress and not to be used to identify which aspects of the cultural commons need to be conserved or used to examine the modern economic and technological forces of enclosure.

If we mistakenly think that the current expressions of individual intelligence are determined by the architecture of the brain or by the embodied experiences of the individual, as George Lakoff and Mark Johnson would have us believe (1999, p. 555), then little attention will be given either to the cultural patterns of thinking that reinforce the idea of the autonomous individual or to the changes that must be made. The languaging processes of a culture are perhaps the most important in ensuring that the thought patterns and daily practices are not too different from what previous generations took for granted. These intergenerational cultural patterns often are individually interpreted in terms of personal biographical experiences, and even misinterpreted—which can lead to minor, and even major, changes over time. In many instances what appear on the surface to be radical changes in intergenerational practices and beliefs, when examined more closely, turn out to be changes that are consistent with the deep cultural assumptions that have been taken for granted for hundreds—even thousands—of years. Examples include the assumptions about an anthropocentric and patriarchal world. The assumptions about being an autonomous individual answerable only to God, to civil law, and now only to oneself, are yet other examples of how past ways of thinking continue in a culture that appears on the surface to be undergoing constant change.

Schools, universities, the media, and the daily languaging processes within families, social organizations, and peer groups inculcate the deepest conceptual patterns of the culture and reinforce the idea that words stand for real things—such as a tree, a landscape, a smile, an aggressive behavior, etc. Youth are particularly vulnerable to being *True.* dependent upon the vocabulary that reproduces the conceptual framework taken for granted by their peers and adults. While there may be fleeting moments of personal experience that do not align with the cultural ways of representing reality, speaking the language and thinking within the linguistically influenced conceptual frameworks acquired in primary socialization reproduce, with little variation, the symbolic heritage of the language community into which they are born. Even highly educated and supposedly cutting-edge thinkers take for granted the deep cultural assumptions (the basis of interpretative frameworks referred to as root metaphors) constituted hundreds of years ago. For example, environmentalists, linguists, and scientists, ranging from E.O. Wilson, George Lakoff, and Richard Dawkins, continue to refer to the brain as a machine, which demonstrates again how the mechanistic root metaphor constituted by western scientists during the early seventeenth century continues to guide thinking in what is considered one of the leading scientific fields of inquiry. Other root metaphors, such as patriarchy, individualism, progress, economism, anthropocentrism, reproduce with only slight modifications the interpretative frameworks that continue to marginalize the patterns of thinking associated with ecological intelligence.

The question that needs to be addressed is how an understanding of the metaphorical nature of most of our words, as well as the role that the culture's root metaphors play in the selection of analogs that frame the meaning of words, such as individualism, wilderness, progress, technology, data, and so forth, challenges the idea that values and moral judgments are a matter of individual reflection and choice. The widely held assumption that individuals choose the values that guide their behavior can be attributed to a combination of cultural traditions that go unexamined in most schools and universities. The Cartesian mind/body separation, along with political arguments about the rights and freedoms of the individual, represent one stream of thinking that has helped create the idea of individuals as being their own moral agents. A second source of influence is the way in which cultural traditions, even those that represent alternatives to dependence upon a consumer lifestyle, are being abstractly represented and framed as being out-of-date, old-fashioned, and impediments to progress. The narratives of a culture that carry forward the moral values that are to guide relationships between humans, and between humans and natural systems, have become part of the cultural amnesia of the more self-centered individuals in society.

The idea of individual autonomy is based on the root metaphor of individualism, which is supported by other root metaphors, such as progress and an anthropocentric world-view. This combination of root metaphors influences which words are consistent in supporting the total explanatory framework. That is, without the assumptions that equate change with a linear form of progress and that this is a human-centered world, the assumption about autonomous individuals would not exist. These and other root metaphors have given rise to conceptually supporting vocabularies that influence which words are to be excluded for threatening the conceptual and moral coherence of the prevailing root metaphors. For example, such words and phrases as tradition (viewed in a positive light), culture, ecologically sustainable, ecological intelligence, post-industrial, and so forth, would not be used as part of a discourse framed by the root metaphors of individualism, progress, and anthropocentrism. Similarly, the root metaphors of mechanism, progress, and individualism (interpreted as being free of cultural influences) that still dominate so much of today's science are now being challenged by such words as consciousness, cultural epistemologies, organic processes, and ecology (with the latter becoming a more prominent part of the language/thought process among some people). For example, leading scientists rely upon mechanistic metaphors to explain the brain's architecture of neural networks but have avoided explaining how differences in cultural epistemologies influence memory, intentionality, and so forth. There is a similar tension between what can and cannot be explained when the theory of evolution is turned into a root metaphor. Are memes really the cultural equivalent to genes, and will the process of natural selection ensure the survival of market liberalism rather than governments based on social justice principles? The outcome of these debates will have an influence not only upon which words (metaphors) are no longer politically correct but also on the moral values that are to be taken for granted. Indeed, some scientists are now arguing that moral values are the result of natural selection.

The important point to be derived from these examples is that language is used to communicate about relationships. *That is, the use of words (metaphors whose meanings were framed by an earlier choice of analogs) communicates how the attributes of the participants in the rela-tionships are to be understood.* The analogs decided upon in the distant past for understanding the attributes of a wilderness, a woman, a desert, an insect, an oral culture, an environment, etc., are the primary and mostly unrecognized moral templates of the culture. If the analogs com-municate that the wilderness has the attribute of being a place of danger, then it is morally appropriate to bring it under human control—which usually means exploiting it for human purposes, such as converting it into a national park, an economic resource, and so forth. Similarly, when the old analogs are used for understanding what women are like, such as intellectually inferior to men, emotional, capable of only certain occupations, then behaviors that reprimand women for being too aggres-sive, too independent, wanting to be an artist, and so forth, are consid-ered moral. If the analogs for understanding a pesticide, such as DDT, includes the attribute of killing insects and other pests, then spreading it across ecologically diverse plant and animal populations is morally justified—in the name of scientific progress and increased profits.

The analogs that frame the meaning of words are often the over-looked source of the moral values that we mistakenly identify as the subjective choice of the individual. While individual reflection and choice do, in fact, lead to moral decisions, the actual scope of such decisions is limited—and varies from individual to individual. One has only to ask, "What are the attributes associated with different words?" to obtain an idea of how much of the individual's moral codes is the result of reflection and personal choice—and how much corresponds to the taken-for-granted moral codes shared by others in the same language community. The largely taken-for-granted status of most of the indi-vidual's moral values is acquired at the same tacit level that characterizes learning the languaging systems of one's culture.

In effect, *learning the language of one's cultural group also involves learning the group's largely taken-for-granted moral codes.* The racism of earlier generations of Anglo and European immigrants was, and still is, the moral template that guides the behavior of many whites toward people of color. Similarly, the language of the Anglo and European im-migrants carried forward the moral templates that still guide the behav-iors and attitudes of millions of Americans toward the environment. The language used to stereotype different ethnic and religious groups, ranging from the Irish, Jews, Mexicans, Chinese, Italians, to indigenous cultures, framed how the attributes of groups of people were understood by members of the dominant culture—and thus what was regarded as morally permissible. To reiterate a key point: Insofar as the analogs settled upon by earlier thinkers continue to frame the meaning of words still taken for granted today, and that the analogs continue to exclude consideration of other attributes, the moral templates inherited from the past perpetuate the problem of relying upon ways of thinking (including the misconceptions and silences) that were responses to the challenges of these earlier eras. If space allowed, it would be easy to demonstrate that many of the analogs that frame the meaning of the words we rely upon today highlight attributes that were supportive of the Industrial Revolution and the creation of a consumer-dependent culture.

There have been recent changes in the attributes linguistically associated with certain social groups. Most public school teachers and university professors responded to the civil rights and feminist movements by recognizing how the racist and sexist language previously taken for granted needed to be revised. This process of revising how the attributes of these groups had been understood for hundreds of years led to identifying analogs that mirrored the current achievements being made by different members of these groups. Given the new and currently validated analogs, it is no longer morally permissible to deny members of these groups access to certain professional fields—such as denying women the right to join combat units in the military and an African American winning the presidency of the United States.

Perhaps one of the most powerful examples of how a group's choice of analogs frames the meaning of words, and thus how the culturally designated attributes of the Other become the basis of widely sanctioned moral behavior, can be seen in how an early English translation of the New Testament changed the names of Yeshua, Shimon Kefa, Shaul, and Miryam to Jesus, Peter, Paul, and Mary. If the early English translators had referred to Jesus as "Rabbi" (which he was), instead of as "Master," perhaps a different moral code might have avoided the centuries-long persecution of the Jews. The English translation emphasized the differences between the Christians and the Jews, rather than the continuities, and the differences opened the door to identifying analogs that encoded the deepest prejudices—which, in turn, led to the moral code that sanctioned the killing fields in industrial Germany and rural Russia, as well as elsewhere.

If classroom teachers and university professors would focus more on the history of words, on how the prevailing root metaphors that provided conceptual direction and moral legitimacy to the industrial/consumer-oriented culture that is now being globalized, and on how mutually supportive root metaphors exclude the use of certain words and assumptions essential to the moral codes of ecologically sustainable cultures, students would be more aware of words that are morally problematic. They would be more likely to be aware of the linguistic basis of colonizing other cultures—which is usually masked by reliance upon metaphors that serve as the god-words within the colonizing culture. Without this awareness, students will continue to take for granted the recursive moral frameworks based on how westerners in the past understood the attributes of people who did not share their social class and skin color, as well as the attributes of the plants and animals that did not have economic value. The hubris that accompanies the strong sense of individualism that the market system requires will keep students from considering the possibility that the moral values they unconsciously have adopted from the past are a primary source of conflict in their relationships with others—and of the sense of struggle they experience in subduing the environment.

Even if public school teachers and university professors were to encourage students to examine the connections between the history of words, and how the deep cultural assumptions that led to the choice of analogs and thus to how the dominant culture continues to understand the attributes of what is being named, the increasing reliance upon the educational uses of computers will largely nullify their efforts. If the analogs settled upon in the distant past are not updated in ways that take account of the cultural and natural ecosystems in which people participate on a daily basis, the moral judgments about how to think and act in these relationships will continue to be based on abstractions handed down from the past.

It is important to reiterate Bateson's insights about the problems connected with the individual's assumption that the socially available conceptual maps are always accurate guides to the territory of daily life—especially when thinking about the cultural-altering characteristics of computers. The increased dependency on computer-mediated learning and communication further exacerbates the problem of abstract thinking, which is a prominent characteristic of individually centered intelligence.

What appears on the screen, whether in the form of narratives, models, visual reproductions, or even direct visual images and voices, is always limited in representing the complexity of local contexts—including the tacit dimensions of culturally mediated embodied experiences. The exercise of ecological intelligence involves not only a state of awareness framed by the background understanding that one is part of interdependent cultural and natural ecologies, but also an awareness of the ongoing differences which make a difference in local contexts and relationships. Ecological intelligence, in short, involves an awareness of the consequences of one's actions on the larger network of cultural and environmental relationships.

What is taken for granted, as well as the tacit aspects of cultural contexts, cannot be fully digitized or represented by the printed word. Furthermore, what is digitized and represented in terms of language systems that can be processed through some form of computer technology becomes separated from its original context. That is, the contextual nature of embodied experiences that can be abstractly represented, and thus capable of being communicated through the internet, is essentially a visual and auditory reality that people around the world can only engage in at a superficial level. The limitations of print-based and computer-mediated learning and communication do not mean that there are no genuine advantages to print-based and computer-mediated learning. Both have many positive advantages, but both also privilege abstract thinking over what can be learned from the changes occurring in local contexts.

The issue that connects this discussion of the increased reliance upon computers to individuals who assume that their moral decisions are personally determined is whether computers continue to reinforce the western print-based tradition of abstract thinking—and thus to accepting without question the moral values encoded in the historically derived analogs that frame the meaning of most words. Computer-mediated thinking and communication reinforce a conduit view of language, which fits a model of communication that is profoundly different from that of face-to-face communication where it is possible for the participants to become aware of the assumptions being taken for granted by the Other. The ability to communicate respect for the Other, while at the same time questioning the assumptions that frame the meaning of the words used by the Other, may result in clarifying how the conceptual history of the words that are the source of misunderstandings can be rectified.

For example, the differences between how the Anglo/Europeans and the indigenous cultures in the so-called New World understood ownership of the land, and the moral decisions between these two profoundly different conceptual frameworks, partly hinged on the differences between a cultural orientation that privileged the authority of the printed word (written contracts, peace agreements, printed maps, etc.) and the oral traditions that connected a people's present with their past. This is not just an example from the colonizing past, with its special ecology of language and moral behavior. These same tensions and power relationships continue to be played out today as corporations and politicians appropriate the land and resources of cultures that are largely based on oral traditions and thus may not have written contracts that establish ownership in the western pattern. Computer-mediated communication simply exacerbates these on-going asymmetrical power relations. The many cultures currently being subjugated by the authority given to abstract thinking, (e.g., the need to exploit the environment of others in the name of progress, development, free market forces, freedom, democracy, and so forth), highlight again the connections between words (metaphors), the culturally and historically derived analogs that frame their meanings (that is, attributes associated with them), and how the assigned attributes frame what constitutes moral behavior.

In the past, differences between the spoken and printed word could be discussed in classrooms where the teacher played a more direct mediating role. With the switch from books to computers, the teacher's role is now more marginalized—especially in being able to raise questions and to provide the relevant historical background information that is missing from the software programs. Given that most classroom teachers and professors still have not given serious attention to the complicit role that language plays in deepening the ecological crisis, the recursive conceptual patterns reinforced by the people who write the educational software, as well as the linguistic patterns that now dominate cyberspace, go largely unnoticed. Educators need to ask whether it is possible to develop the students' moral responsibility toward the natural world if the language represents species as abstractions having only negative qualities—such as being a weed or as a pest. What are the historical connotations associated with such names as snake, wolf, killer whale, bat, plant, etc.? Does the printed name of a plant, such as "rhododendron," which people in the Pacific Northwest use to beautify their yards, obscure the important distinction between native and non-native plants—and the ecological, and thus moral, implications of assuming that it can be introduced into any environment? Again, the issue of words, analogs, and attributes, and what they conceptually and morally hide, comes up. The individual's exercise of her/his own intelligence is likely to be driven by wanting a specific outcome, whereas the exercise of ecological intelligence involves understanding a plant in terms of its relationships within a larger web of information and energy exchanges. Computers may be able to model the latter, but this process is still limited to marginalizing the ecological wisdom gained through the intergenerational memory of the culture.

There is another question that needs to be asked; namely, does the ability of computers to model the behavior of ecological systems overcome the instrumental and experimental orientation towards learning that comes close to what Aldo Leopold describes as a "land ethic"? In *A Sand County Almanac*, Leopold recounts the transformative change in his consciousness that resulted from looking into the eyes of a dying wolf which he had shot while acting out his role as an agent of civilization and thereby governed by the moral codes that specified how to deal with the dangers of wildness. And what could be a greater symbol of wildness and danger than a wolf surrounded by a half dozen nearly grown pups? He recounts that transformation of consciousness and of the old moral code in the following:

> We reached the old wolf in time to watch a fierce green fire dying in her eyes. I realized then, and have known ever since, that there was something new to me in those eyes—something known only to her and to the mountain. I was young then, and full of trigger-itch; I thought that because fewer wolves meant more deer, that no wolves would mean a hunter's paradise. But after seeing the green fire fade, I sensed that neither the wolf nor the mountain agreed with such a view. (1960, p. 130)

He goes on to articulate what he regards as an essential extension of how we should understand the parameters of our moral responsibilities. As Leopold puts it: "A thing is right when it tends to preserve the integrity, stability, and beauty of the biotic community. It is wrong when it tends otherwise." (pp. 224–225) This moral imperative led him to suggest changes in the analogs associated with words, such as "community." In place of understanding community as a physical space within which humans live and interact as workers, consumers, and as autonomous moral agents, Leopold suggests that a land ethic should enlarge "the boundaries of the community to include soils, water, plants and animals, or collectively: the land.... In short, a land ethic changes the role of *Homo sapiens* from conqueror of the land-community to plain member and citizen of it. It implies respect for his fellow-members, and also respect for the community as such." (p. 204) It is important to note that Leopold's radical change in consciousness that led to his expanded understanding of community did not come from abstract thinking. Indeed, when he shot the wolf he still took for granted the old conceptual/moral maps which had been handed down through the formal educational process he underwent, and reinforced by his contemporaries.

Becoming aware of the different forms of intelligence exercised in other cultures, especially cultures that have learned to live within the limits and possibilities of their bioregions while at the same time developing complex symbolic worlds, may help us recognize more easily the taken-for-granted assumptions that lead so many Westerners, and especially our intellectual elites, to act out the myth that we are autonomous individuals—uninfluenced by the past, needing only to rely upon our immediate subjective judgments and the power of critical thinking.

Keith Basso's study of the ecological intelligence of the Western Apache is important as it brings out an entirely different set of cultural influences—including the Apache's deliberate effort to develop the disciplined way of thinking that leads to "wisdom." As an anthropologist, Basso studied how their land ethic was intergenerationally passed along through the place-based narratives of their ancestors. His experience with the Apache ranchers living near Cibecue, Arizona, led to conversations that yielded important insights into their form of consciousness. These experiences, along with observing how members of the community recalled the place-based stories of their ancestors as an indirect way of bringing to the attention of a youth, who had acted in an environmentally disruptive way, the moral values that should have guided his behavior, led Basso to recognize a profoundly different cultural approach to the development of ecological intelligence—which the Apache understood as wisdom. Wisdom, as he discovered through careful listening and observation of Apache interactions, is achieved through the development of three mental attributes. These include cultivating the qualities of "smoothness, resilience, and steadiness" of mind, which Basso explains in the following way:

> Mental smoothness is believed by the Apache to be the product of two subsidiary conditions—mental resilience and mental steadiness—which ward off distractions that interfere with calm and focused attention. These distractions are grouped into two broad classes according to whether their sources are external or internal to the individual.... While resilience of mind contributes to mental smoothness by blunting the effects of external distractions, 'steadiness of mind' accomplishes this objective by removing the sources of internal ones. (1996, p. 132)

Basso notes that what the Apache understand as steadiness of mind requires relinquishing feelings of superiority and aggressiveness toward others. He also notes that "Steady minds are unhampered by feelings of arrogance or pride, anger or vindictiveness, jealousy or lust—all of which present serious hindrances to calm and measured thinking" (p. 133). Comparing the mental/moral qualities of wisdom valued, but not always attained, within Apache culture with the qualities of mind that Bateson considers to be obstacles to the development of ecological intelligence is useful for bringing into focus the daunting challenge associated with the dominant patterns of thinking in the West.

Neither the Quechua nor the Western Apache, while very different in their approaches to ecological intelligence, are encumbered by the recursive assumptions and silences of mythopoetic narratives and philosophers whose abstractions were never informed by an awareness of the need to align cultural practices with the actual characteristics of the local cultural and natural ecologies. Nor is the Quechua and the Western Apache ability to read the changes occurring in natural systems, and to adapt their practices accordingly, held hostage to earlier misconceptions encoded in the language that western thinkers still mistakenly assume to be accurate guides for imposing their progressive and materialistic agendas on the cultural and natural ecosystems that are in various stages of collapse. As subsistence cultures, the Quechua and the Western Apache are able to avoid the double binds created by an industrial/consumer-dependent culture that equates progress with exploiting and contaminating what remains of the earth's resources. Unfortunately, the youth of both cultures are coming more under the influence of modern technologies and values. Thus, whether their traditions of exercising ecological intelligence survive beyond the current generation is very much in doubt. *yikes* These two cultures, as well as other subsistence cultures, are under pressure from the forces of modernization, such as public schools, media exposure to false pictures of life in a consumer culture, technologies, such as computers and cell phones, and international political pressure to engage in economic development that will replace their local cultural commons with shopping malls and the abstract thinking that is the hallmark of cyberspace.

Within a western context, ecological intelligence is exercised in many situations where individuals are mentally present, relying upon all the senses, and responding to the differences which make a difference while being mindful of the consequences that follow their responses. Marriages and friendships depend upon partners exercising ecological intelligence. Farmers, artists, and many others exercise ecological intelligence by giving attention and responding to the changes occurring in the natural systems and the materials with which they are working. The exercise of ecological intelligence in daily life occurs when responses to differences are not dictated by rigid plans and formulaic thinking. Giving attention to the differences which make a difference is an essential part of playing a game of tennis, sailing in difficult wind conditions, preparing a meal, holding an intelligent conversation. It is exercised in many aspects of daily life—but is not present when individual intelligence of preconceived plans, explanations, hubris, and reified ideas and values take over as the dominating forces. What separates an ecological and individual intelligence approach to moral values is that the former requires the awareness of the interdependent relationships where the impact on the Other has a reciprocal impact on oneself. The individually centered approach to moral values is oriented in ways that make moral values a matter of determining what is in the interest of the individual. The sense of being autonomous is accompanied by a sense of indifference to the well-being of the Other—whether it is another person or the environment. Many of the people who are addicted to consumerism and who unquestioningly embrace the ethos of a modern, competitive, get-ahead-at-all-cost lifestyle possess many of the characteristics of a sociopath —having the same destructive impact on the natural ecologies that sociopaths have on the cultural ecologies they exploit.

It is ironic that most classroom teachers and university professors, especially in the social sciences, humanities, and professional schools, such as education and business, are indifferent to the need to revise the conceptual patterns they learned from their mentors who were promoters of the modernizing cultural agenda. Those relying upon the tradition of academic freedom to justify their indifference to examining the cultural roots of the ecological crisis have resulted in universities, and the school teachers they educate, becoming increasingly aligned with the reactionary elements in society who are also in denial that there is an ecological crisis. Their complicity in passing on the mind-set that is exacerbating the ecological crisis on a global scale is especially troubling as these educational institutions are the only real hope, beyond that of the local cultural commons in which adults are beginning to engage in practices that contribute to local self-sufficiency.

Assuming that faculty can become aware of how their past socialization is a source of double bind thinking, what educational reforms should they introduce? Briefly, the reforms should include:

1. Introducing students to the language issues discussed here—that words have a history and that the attributes historically associated with the meaning of the words carry forward many of the culture's moral values;

2. Having students undertake auto-ethnographies as they experience the differences between individual and ecological intelligence (including helping students to recognize when they are exercising both forms)—and the consequences in terms of the larger cultural and natural ecologies in which they participate;

3. Studying cultures that have developed forms of ecological intelligence suited to their bioregions;

4. After acquiring an understanding of the differences between orality and literacy (which means reading the research findings of Jack Goody, Eric Havelock, and Walter Ong), examining the forms of intelligence computers reinforce—and the forms of knowledge they marginalize; and

5. Encouraging students to become observers of the many ways in which individual autonomy is being reinforced by the media, in the classroom, and in other social venues.

CHAPTER 6

How the Classroom Uses of Computers Undermine Ecological Intelligence

Many of the world's people, as well as most institutions and businesses, are now dependent upon the use of computers. Thus, the following explanation of how computers undermine ecological intelligence should not be interpreted as a blanket indictment of this technology. Rather, the focus here is on how the increasing reliance upon computer-mediated learning in formal educational settings, such as public schools and universities, promotes the western tradition of assuming that intelligence is an attribute of the individual who is culturally driven to achieve greater autonomy. The focus is also on the technological limitations of computer technology, such as the inability to digitize the symbolically layered nature of local contexts, as well as the inability of computer programmers to explicitly recognize how what they take for granted promotes abstract thinking. Given the historical influences of print, some degree of abstract thinking is unavoidable; indeed, it is useful when used to make explicit the nature of culturally grounded experiences, and when it is used to guide certain behaviors and activities, such as working in local contexts to achieve social and eco-justice. Abstract thinking that takes the form of theory, especially when it is informed by an understanding of the relationships between local and global systems, is also essential to developing less ecologically damaging technologies and in recognizing the conceptual errors of previous generations. The problem is when abstract thinking becomes the dominant pattern of thinking. It then marginalizes awareness of the "differences which make a difference" within the local contexts that are the basis of the information exchanges that prompt the changes circulating through all levels of the natural and cultural ecologies.

Bateson's conceptual framework enables us to avoid the ecologically destructive assumptions of the previous theorists who have been taken seriously as educational and social reformers, including the theorists who have provided the social justice arguments that support the current idea that every child should be equipped with a personal computer. His conceptual framework will be used here as the primary source for making explicit why computer-mediated learning is a major obstacle to making the transition from individual to ecological intelligence. While computer technology has now become integrated with other media, such as voice, video, and face-to-face communication with others over vast distances, its dominant mode of knowledge storage, retrieval, and communication remains based on the age-old tradition of print and other systems of abstract representation. It is, therefore, important to bring into the analysis of the cultural amplification and reduction characteristics of computer-mediated learning the insights of scholars, such as Jack Goody, Eric Havelock, and Walter Ong.

Their basic argument is that, even when cultural variables are taken into account, orality (the spoken word, reliance upon narratives, and other forms of face-to-face communication, such as dance and ceremonies), organizes consciousness in ways that are profoundly different from print-based thinking and communication. These differences are especially significant when considering whether technologically mediated forms of knowledge take account of local contexts—that is, an awareness of the immediate context where the differences which make a difference (or as Foucault puts it, "an action upon an action") affect ongoing relationships and interdependencies. Orality involves all the senses, whether it takes the form of a narrative (which is itself a performance), a face-to-face encounter, or a mentoring relationship. Print-based communication and experience, on the other hand, rely upon sight (reading the word and viewing the images), and make what is present to the other senses (including sound) not only irrelevant but also unwanted distractions. Writing and reading are primarily solitary activities—though as Ong points out, electronic communication (cell phones, texting, online games, Skype-based communication, etc.), creates some of the conditions he refers to as "secondary orality" (1982, pp. 136–137).

The most prominent example of secondary orality is the experience of participating in an online community of shared interest—even though the participants may never meet face-to-face and may even be communicating through their avatars. There are other differences between orality and literacy that need to be considered in assessing how computer-mediated learning reinforces abstract thinking. The printed word, unlike the dynamic nature of the spoken word, presents the fixed reality of a text that allows an analysis of differences in written accounts. It thus provides the fixed, though not always accurate, reference points for critical thinking—which have had demonstrable benefits throughout human history. Yet the limitations of print-dominated thinking can be see in the Janus nature of today's computer technology. During the era of western colonization, print-based abstract thinking led to written documents and the drawing of lines on maps that represented the boundaries of what were to be new western-style countries with centralized governments. Unfortunately, reliance upon abstract thinking failed to take account of local ethnic differences, including how these different ethnic groups settled territorial disputes. This legacy is now the source of seemingly unending international conflicts. The current efforts to promote democracy, individualism, and free markets, without considering the local cultural traditions in which these western abstractions are to be introduced, further adds to the problems. Yet another example of abstract thinking can be seen in the current use of political labels, which again reflects an indifference to historical context and local experience.

Other differences that separate cultures based primarily upon the spoken word from those that store more of their knowledge in the abstract medium of print can be seen in the role that mentors play in oral cultures in comparison to the vast numbers of printed manuals and the current ways of measuring intelligence in western cultures. In oral cultures, intelligence is demonstrated through performance, while in western cultures, where print has been the dominant mode of cultural storage, intelligence is measured by the number of correct responses to questions in which no knowledge of local contexts is required. The connections between knowledge and culturally embodied performance are thus separated—which too often has led to upholding the importance of abstract ideas (such as profits, victory, freedom, etc.)—while at the same time destroying the viability of the local natural and cultural systems. A difference often overlooked is ways in which oral cultures update their narratives in ways that take account of changes in the life of the community, while printed records, by their very nature, are static. Anyone who has written an article or book, or had someone else explain in print her/his state of thinking, cannot help being aware of how the printed account quickly becomes a storage site of inaccurate information.

There are other differences noted by Ong, Havelock, and Goody.

One is that orality leads to personality structures that are communal and externally oriented. Literacy, on the other hand, fosters more introspective personalities, a desire for autonomy, and, as we are now witnessing in the West, seeking one's personal interests over those of the community. These are rough comparisons that are affected by a myriad of cultural differences, but the basic differences between the spoken and printed word need to be assessed in terms of which mode of communication and storage takes account of local contexts—which I have argued in previous chapters is an important characteristic of ecological intelligence. These differences are also important in terms of whether such key metaphors as "tradition," "emancipation," "transformation," "modernization," and "development" are treated as abstractions that guide behaviors and reform agendas, regardless of cultural and environmental contexts, or are understood as examples of the abstract thinking of earlier generations who associated orality with "illiteracy" and thus cultural backwardness.

Before returning to the main focus of this chapter—namely, what Bateson's conceptual framework helps us understand about the connections between computer-mediated learning and the marginalization of the importance of local contexts—it is important to emphasize a point that Eric Havelock makes about one of the many advantages gained through print. In *The Muse Learns to Write*, he observes that in oral cultures there may be members whose thinking goes against the orthodoxies held by the community. Print allows the possibility of preserving those ideas and values to be discovered by future generations who have developed to the point where the genuine merits of those ideas can be recognized. Print, in effect, allows the participants in a community to gain distance from the flow of taken-for-granted experiences sustained through oral communication, and thus to be able to reflect on what needs to be changed or conserved.

However, when print becomes the primary mode for understanding the living traditions of the community, it turns those traditions into abstractions that lack the depth of actual experience. The living nature of communal memory, which may not always meet today's standards of social justice, is also lost through reliance on print. While often taken for granted, these living traditions—which range from sharing a meal, performing a skill, such as weaving, participating in a political debate, being mentored, sharing a task, (and in many cultures, exploiting others)—involve all the senses and are the basis of memories and self-identity.

Print erases all of this and leads the reader into the realm of sweeping generalizations that are easily framed by modernizing ideologies. Unfortunately, what the proponents of today's modernizing ideologies have achieved is the widely held practice of ignoring, as Havelock puts it, that "tradition in short is taught by action, not by idea or principle" (1986, p. 77). It is the culturally mediated embodied experience that should be the focus of attention, rather than the reductionist ideological agenda of the writer or programmer of educational simulation programs. As educational reformers become aware of how the abstract ideas promoted by western philosophers and educational theorists are also shared by the proponents of globalizing the free-market ideology and consumer-dependent lifestyle, they will face the challenge of becoming aware of the traditions they have been socialized to reject as obstacles to progress and individual freedom. Then the critical questions will be: Which traditions strengthen the mutual support systems within the community and help to avoid a lifestyle that has an ecologically unsustainable carbon and toxic footprint? and, Which traditions are deepening the ecological crisis? These are also the fundamental questions that need to be asked of the current practice of promoting computer-mediated learning in classrooms around the world.

Using Gregory Bateson's Conceptual Framework for Understanding How Computer-Mediated Learning Promotes the Same Mind-Set that Underlies the Ecological Crisis

The earlier chapters explored how Bateson's conceptual framework illuminates many of the basic misconceptions inherited from the past that educators continue to promote as the latest expressions of progress. It was also used to examine the educational reforms that need to be undertaken if we are to have a sustainable future. As explained earlier, Bateson's five key insights have particular relevance for challenging the traditionalist and social reform thinking about the role of a public school and university education. That is, they provide an alternative perspective on the cultural reproduction characteristics of computer-mediated learning. Again, it needs to be kept in mind that the digitized forms of cultural reproduction that are being made explicit and criticized here should not be interpreted as a blanket rejection of all educational uses of computers. As in the earlier chapters, the effort to understand how ecological intelligence is exercised in different cultural contexts, and in using different technologies, is only an introduction to a complex set of relationships—the ecological crisis, the increased reliance upon print-based technologies, the challenge facing different cultures to recover (if that is still possible) their less consumer-dependent traditions, and how to make the transition whereby more aspects of daily life are based on ecological intelligence. Hopefully, others will begin to focus on these relationships, the educational reforms that take them into account, and the constructive role that a more limited use of computers can play.

How Computer-Mediated Learning Promotes the Recursive Western Epistemology that Was Constituted Before There Was an Awareness of Environmental Limits

As explained earlier, when the repetition of a culture's patterns of thinking, such as thinking of separate entities, linear progress, and the objective nature of knowledge, etc., are recognized as examples of recursive thinking, the modern idea that change is a progressive force that frees people from the influence of traditions can then be more easily questioned. The idea of progress itself is a recursive pattern of thinking that goes back nearly five centuries. This and other important features of the western modernizing epistemology, such as thinking of the individual as autonomous, technology as a tool and thus culturally neutral, a human-centered world, language as a conduit in a sender/receiver process of communication, etc., also have their origins deep in the mythopoetic and evocative experiences of the distant past. Yet, few classroom teachers and professors are aware of the recursive nature of what they represent to students as the latest expression of progressive thinking. What is hidden from students is that the root metaphors that underlie modern and progressive patterns of thinking have their origins in the distant past. For example, one of the more prominent recursive conceptual patterns is to think of print-encoded knowledge as the expression of an advanced culture and to think of oral cultures as backward and victims of "illiteracy." This recursive pattern also includes giving high-status to abstract thinking while regarding local contexts as having little relevance for judging the veracity of abstract knowledge. The tendency to universalize the meaning of what appears in print has played an important role in the colonizing of other cultures. Reliance upon print-based knowledge has also helped to denigrate the importance of the intergenerational knowledge acquired from place-based experiences and passed along through face-to-face relationships.

Bateson's insight that our modern progressive culture sustains itself, while introducing minor variations on the core conceptual patterns, by reproducing the silences and misconceptions of earlier eras has particular relevance for demystifying the widely held belief that computer-based technologies are a real break from the past. This assumption, which few educators are able to question, has two major consequences. The first is that educators in public schools and universities ignore the historical origins of the cultural conceptual patterns reinforced by the use of computers—that is, the cultural patterns that are not obvious to the person focused on the computer screen. The result is that students are not encouraged to reflect on the ways in which the recursive cultural patterns of thinking reinforced by the use of the computer contribute to ecologically unsustainable lifestyles.

To list the patterns reinforced by the very nature of the technology, even as it is undergoing seemingly fundamental transformations that incorporate voice and visual life-like representations, could, and indeed should, become a major focus of the curriculum. For example, what cultural missteps have resulted from privileging print over voice? Was the privileging of print over oral traditions a factor in viewing oral cultures as backward and primitive? Was print an essential feature of the contracts and treaties that established the ownership of the territories of oral cultures? How does print-mediated learning contribute to marginalizing the importance of being aware of local contexts (ecologies) where the differences which make a difference occur? Do the long-held assumptions about the empowering nature of the rational process, as well as the idea of a linear form of progress, retard understanding natural and cultural systems as interdependent ecologies? What are the long-term consequences of the degradation of habitats and the inability of species to renew themselves? Does print-based knowledge really contrib- *Imp.* ute to the individual's freedom, or has it functioned as a way for the *Question* state to expand its authority? If we consider the transition from relatively self-sufficient communities to an increasing dependence upon corporations that require increasing profits and political control, do the computer-based surveillance systems corporations increasingly rely upon contribute to the freedom of individuals? The internet is considered by many people, including students, as enhancing freedom of choice and control over time, yet their activities are encoded as data that is often sold to various corporate interests. Is this really an expansion of freedom?

Given the complexity of the cultural patterns of thinking reinforced by the nature of computer technologies, and by the taken-for-granted patterns of thinking of the people who use computers (which correspond to the silences and cultural-mediating characteristics of the technology itself), the question arises about whether computer-mediated learning becomes a major obstacle to the development of ecological intelligence. There have been gains over time in reframing the nature of the individual's attributes—with some prejudices being disapproved by the larger society. The overriding reality, however, is that the long hours youth devote to using computers and related technologies, which seemingly provide unlimited choices, reinforce the illusion of being an autonomous individual. Yet, it is a false sense of autonomy. Being primarily dependent upon only two of the physical senses, the reliance on the sight and sound connected with the technologically mediated experience, leads to ignoring face-to-face relationships, as well as the interactions occurring in the surrounding natural and cultural systems.

The second consequence of assuming that computer-mediated learning is superior to face-to-face interaction with a teacher is that another characteristic of the West's dominant and age-old pattern of thinking asserts itself. This is the messianic tradition shared by most Christian religions, corporations, politicians, and educators—all of whom justify their efforts to convert the peoples of the world to adopt western values, patterns of thinking, and consumer habits on the basis of their supposed superior development. The current effort to make a computer available to every child, regardless of her/his culture, is the latest expression of this messianic impulse that is deeply rooted in the psychic and pocketbook interests of mainstream Americans. What is hidden is how the culturally mediating characteristics of computers represent yet another approach to colonizing other cultures to the western patterns of thinking. Largely unnoticed, except by the parents and grandparents in cultures that are still largely orally based, are the recursive conceptual traditions of the West that are being promoted behind the façade of a supposedly culturally neutral technology.

The classroom uses of computers in Peru, China, India, and in countries across Africa and the Middle East—to cite the diversity of cultures that are making the use of computers a key part of their approaches to educational reforms—tacitly reinforce a print-based form of consciousness that marginalizes the intergenerational knowledge previously passed along through face-to-face communication. While the cultural differences in intergenerational knowledge range widely in terms of what strengthens moral reciprocity and sustainable practices within the community, and what perpetuates exploitive and discriminatory practices, the privileging of print-based abstract thinking that enables students to communicate globally with other abstract thinkers involves a loss of the local knowledge, skills, and mentoring relationships that are far more complex than what can be recovered in digitized form.

Other recursive patterns of thinking in the West that are being passed along through the use of computers include the following assumptions: that technological changes are an inherently progressive force; that students can access a vast store of information and thus construct their own individualized approach to knowledge; that technology is culturally neutral; that language is a conduit in a sender/receiver process of communicating objective information and data; and, that what is hidden by this technology, namely, the taken-for-granted patterns of thinking of the people who write the educational software programs, does not merit attention. In effect, what is understood as becoming computer literate does not involve a critical examination of the form of cultural colonization that accompanies the use of computers. Nor is any consideration given to how computer-mediated thinking and communicating are undermining the local traditions of ecological intelligence that have been acquired through generations of giving close attention to the interdependencies and life-cycle patterns within the local bioregion— and how they are affected by local cultural practices.

How Understanding the Differences Between the Map and the Territory Illuminate Another Hidden Influence of Computer-Mediated Thinking and Communicating

The phrase "the map is not the territory" also has special relevance for making explicit another characteristic of computer-mediated thinking and learning. As pointed out in an earlier chapter, the map—which most people assume provides an accurate representation of the main features of the territory (such as roads, noteworthy geographical features, rest stops, etc.)—is a cultural construct that represents the mix of silences, taken-for-granted beliefs, culturally derived interpretative frameworks, and experiences of the person who creates the map. Thus, the territory is never fully and accurately represented—especially when language is being used for political purposes. It is important to note that Bateson and Korzybski are not thinking of the relationship between the map and the territory in conventional terms, such as how people think about and use maps in reaching an unfamiliar destination. Nor are they thinking about the political uses of maps. Rather, they use this metaphor as a way of clarifying the current influence of metaphors framed by the choice of analogs in the distant or near past on the conceptual frameworks used to address today's problems.

The basic reason that the maps (conceptual frameworks) are unable to accurately account for the characteristics of the territory (the differences which make a difference that are the basic units of information that prompt changes in the behavior of the participants in the natural and cultural systems) is that they are based on the metaphorical thinking of people who are, in some instances, generations—or even thousands of years—removed from the current natural and cultural ecological systems. Throughout the earlier chapters, examples were given of how the metaphors framed in an earlier era by the choice of analogs that made sense then—such as individualism, tradition, freedom, technology, progress, etc.—represent a form of linguistic colonization of the present by the past. That is, earlier ways of understanding that did not take account of current contexts are being relied upon for understanding how to respond to the cultural roots of the ecological crisis that these earlier patterns of thinking are partly responsible for creating. To put this double bind in Bateson's language: The maps (conceptual frameworks derived from the past) are mistakenly being taken as accurate guides for thinking about the territory (the current mix of cultural and environmental crises).

So how does the problem of the linguistic colonization of the present by the past relate to the educational uses of computers? How does it help us to understand another way in which the classroom uses of computers promote individual rather than ecological intelligence? As pointed out earlier, one of the dominant ways students are socialized to think about the nature and role of language is to view it as a conduit in a sender/receiver process of communication. This way of thinking about language is essential to supporting the myth of objective information and data. It is also essential for supporting the assumption that the rational process is free of cultural influences—and by extension, that intelligence is an attribute of the autonomous individual. Careful observation of how students interact with computers, engage in texting, and even in face-to-face computer-mediated communication, will reveal how they take for granted the conduit view of language. That is, there may be negotiations about how words are being used, but what seldom occurs, especially in classroom settings, is a discussion of the metaphorical nature of words and the history of the process of analogic thinking that is the basis of their current meanings.

As it is now widely assumed that computer-mediated thinking and learning require less teacher/professor involvement in the students' education, there is even less possibility that students will be aware that the printed words appearing on the screen, and in the digitized visual programs, reflect older patterns of thinking and culturally specific assumptions. Students are unlikely to learn that words are metaphors, that they have a history, and that they may be the very metaphors that are undermining their prospects for meaningful work—such as promoting automation as the expression of progress even though automation reduces the need for workers. And, students are likely to be unaware of the metaphors that justified introducing thousands of toxic chemicals into the environment. The argument that is likely to be made in response to this critique of computer-mediated learning is that few classroom teachers and professors engage students in discussions that challenge the conduit view of language. Granted, there is little difference between the silences shared by the people who write the educational software programs and the silences perpetuated by classroom teachers and professors. While they are all complicit in reproducing the silences and misconceptions that characterized their own education, the reliance on computers increases the likelihood that students will continue to ignore that the meaning of the words appearing on the screen are cultural constructions that reflect earlier ways of thinking. That the words appear in print on a computer screen further abstracts them from their originating historical and cultural contexts.

On the positive side, the educational uses of computers can provide students with important information about the loss of habitats, the impacts of global warming on environments and people, and ways of modeling the environmental impacts of human behavior. As demonstrated by the classroom simulation programs SimLife and SimEarth, students also learn how differences in the behavior of one system affect the behavior and even the sustainability of other systems. For all their merits and good intentions, both simulation programs are especially interesting as they provide an example of the map/territory problem that is likely to go unnoticed if the teacher shares the same cultural assumptions as the people who created the programs.

The promotional statement for the SimEarth program starts out with the promise that it will enable students to understand that the "planet as a whole: life, climate, atmosphere, and the planet itself—from dirt and rock to the molten core—all affect each other." The statement goes on to explain that SimEarth can be played in two modes: game and experimental.

> In *game* mode, *you* [the student] will try to develop, manage, and preserve your planet within allotted energy budgets. In *experimental* mode, you will be given unlimited energy to mold *your* planet. This allows *you* to set up any type of planet in any stage of development, and then to introduce any new factors *you* want, and to see what happens.... A single planet can be populated by billions and billions of SimEarthlings. Their welfare is in *your* hands. (1991, p. 2)

This well-intended effort to introduce students to how the "differences which make a difference" influence the patterns that connect, and the interdependent relationships within natural ecosystems, has a major drawback. That is, the recursive patterns of thinking that were major contributors to the degradation of natural systems are reinforced in how the role of students' decision-making is explained—they have been italicized in the above quotation. The three most prominent cultural assumptions that are likely to go unnoticed by most teachers and students include the recursive patterns of thinking of a human-centered world (exemplified in the many ways the students are represented as being in control of natural systems), thinking of humans as living in an experimental relationship with natural systems, and the assumption that experimentation leads to progress in the ability to control natural systems.

In effect, the pattern of thinking reinforced in this software program is really no different from the way of thinking of the chemists who adopted the experimental approach to creating thousands of synthetic chemicals, and then, in the name of progress, introducing them into the environment without understanding their impacts on the genetic behavior of other natural systems. Only later did we learn of the life-disrupting effects of these so-called progressive scientific achievements. Unfortunately, the effects of these poisons will continue to disrupt life-forming processes for years to come. The recursive conceptual frameworks that classroom teachers and educational software programmers learned from their ecologically and linguistically unaware professors continue to be passed along to students who too often lack the matrix of culturally embodied experiences, culturally grounded theory, and ecologically informed language necessary for questioning the misconceptions and silences of earlier generations.

The Connections Between Bateson's Understanding of Double Bind Thinking and His Recommendation that Educational Reforms Engage Students in Level III Learning

Briefly, double bind thinking occurs when what is taken to be progress, such as returning to the former level of full employment which sustained a state of hyper-consumerism, has the effect of further degrading the self-renewing capacity of natural systems. Other examples of double bind thinking include: spending several hundred-thousand dollars for a high-status education when the employment opportunities necessary for repaying loans of this magnitude are disappearing as a result of corporate outsourcing, downsizing, and the relentless drive to replace workers with automated machines; promoting the progressive patterns of thinking that are based on the same deep cultural assumptions that underlie the individually centered consumer lifestyle that serves the interests of the corporations that have put profits ahead of an ecologically sustainable future; relying upon the thought patterns of earlier thinkers who were unaware of environmental limits—especially when these earlier patterns of thinking are at the root of the ecological crisis; promoting approaches to environmental education that fail to take account of the cultural roots of the ecological crisis, and so forth.

Consideration of the different facets of Bateson's thinking, as discussed in previous chapters, clarifies the connections between language, conceptual ways of knowing, and by extension, the differences between individual and ecological intelligence. To reiterate a key point, individual intelligence is fostered by Level II thinking and forms of socialization that reinforce reliance upon context-free, and thus abstract, metaphors. Level II learning and thinking de-emphasize the need to assess the historical origins or to consider the ecological implications of using seemingly context-free metaphors, such as individualism, free markets, development, progress, objective data, etc. Computer-mediated learning has the same limitations, which results from the inability to digitize the tacit and culturally mediated embodied experiences, as well as the taken-for-granted cultural patterns.

As more of the curriculum is being mediated by the cultural orientations reinforced by computers, such as the emphasis on print and other abstract forms of cultural reproduction, and as most of the educational software is created by individuals who still think of language as a conduit for communicating facts, information, and visual images, there is little likelihood that computer-mediated learning will engage students in Level III learning. The current political and economic climate that is leading to educational reforms based on common national core standards, where achievement levels can be measured and teachers held accountable, will mean teaching to the tests. This emphasis will help perpetuate the long-standing indifference on the part of teacher education faculty, and the vast majority of classroom teachers, to the fact that the deepening ecological crisis has its roots partly in the languaging processes that reproduce the same cultural assumptions and silences that gave conceptual direction and moral legitimacy to the industrial culture and free-market system that were guided by the myth of unending progress—and not by any awareness, until the last few years, of environmental limits.

The establishment of national core curriculum standards will lead to viewing computers as the most effective way of introducing these reforms—and measuring whether the prescribed standards have been met. This will further de-emphasize the importance of the local knowledge that sustains the cultural commons. What is not recognized by politicians and most educators in positions of power is that the industrial approach to educational reform cannot accommodate a key feature of Level III learning. That is, if students are to begin thinking about the deep conceptual basis of the current crisis, as well as the lifestyle and community-centered alternatives to a consumer and industrial-dependent existence, it will be necessary for face-to-face relationships between the students and a teacher who understands the dynamics of the linguistic colonization of consciousness as well as the history of the recursive intellectual traditions that are now undermining the survival of future generations. It is in the immediate moments of these face-to-face interactions that teachers need to be able to help students identify and reframe the meaning of words by identifying analogs that are ecologically and culturally informed.

Face-to-face relationships enable the teacher to recognize the taken-for-granted patterns in the students' thinking, in the curriculum materials, and in the media that play an increasing role in misleading the public into thinking that science and technology will be our salvation. Face-to-face relationships between teachers and students are necessary for making explicit and encouraging discussions of the cultural roots of the ecological crisis. Computer-mediated learning can never represent the living contexts in which teaching and learning occur, the students' taken-for-granted patterns of thinking and values, the specific questions that should be asked, and the historical perspective that needs to be introduced at key moments in classroom discussions. Nor can it provide a substitute for the wisdom acquired by reflective teachers who have developed the ability to be aware of, and to learn from, the natural and cultural ecologies in which they have participated in over their more extended lifetime. Regardless of the attempts to mitigate one of the dominant features of print-based technologies—that is, the asymmetrical power relationship between the computer-mediated learning experience and the students—the technology will never be developed to the point where it can replicate the genuine dialog that occurs between teachers who exercise ecological intelligence and students who are beginning to question the connections between current ways of thinking and the ecological crisis.

CHAPTER 7

Educational Reforms that Foster Ecological Intelligence

There are powerful forces of resistance that must be acknowledged when introducing the educational reforms that foster ecological intelligence. The foremost source of resistance is the paradigm gap that now separates the generations. That is, the vast majority of university professors, classroom teachers—and thus the general public that has been educated by them—were socialized to take for granted many of the conceptual underpinnings that supported the idea that intelligence is the attribute that is the basis of individual autonomy. This includes, as mentioned earlier, all the misconceptions that marginalize the awareness that the languaging processes carry forward the misconceptions and silences of earlier eras—including the moral values and deep cultural assumptions rooted in the West's anthropocentric traditions of thinking.

This legacy of late twentieth-century thinking continues to frame today's political discourse where a large majority of the public is in deep denial that the ecological crisis will require fundamental lifestyle changes. Scientists and politicians who take the crisis seriously assume that it can be solved by introducing more energy-efficient and less carbon-producing technologies. The small number of faculty in the social sciences, and the even smaller number in the humanities, who are introducing their students to environmental issues mostly focus on environmental writers, such as Holmes Rolston III, Warwick Fox, Arne Naess, J. Baird Callicott, Aldo Leopold, Wendell Berry—and ecofeminists, such as Charlene Spretnak, Susan Griffin, Carolyn Merchant, Val Plumwood, and Vandana Shiva. These writers are important as they challenge, from different perspectives, the dominant myth of a human-centered and patriarchal world. Reading them contributes to a change of consciousness, but they do not provide students with the knowledge and skills necessary for living lifestyles that are less dependent upon consumerism, or on a less individually centered form of consciousness. Little if any attention is given to discussing with students how the new digital tech-nologies, valued chiefly for their personal convenience, speed, and social networking, perpetuate the same cultural patterns that further marginal-ize awareness of the ecological crisis.

Other obstacles to introducing educational reforms that foster greater reliance upon ecological intelligence include the deepening cul-ture wars in which a mix of religious fundamentalism, and years of a fragmented educational process that leaves students to graduate with only a surface knowledge of the history of ideas, lead to the current violence-prone political discourse. This discourse, which continually degenerates into making the false distinction between friends and enemies, is dominated by an Orwellian mix of political slogans. Labeling as "conservative" the groups that, in the name of patriotism, are under-mining our traditions of civil rights, as well as promoting the elimination of all governmental regulation of the free-market, is evidence of the need for a radical rethinking of which traditions of knowledge are essential to making the transition to an ecologically sustainable future.

The recursive intellectual traditions survive primarily because of institutional rigidity and the unwillingness of tenured faculty to acknowledge that what they take to be cutting-edge thinking in their discipline may not be useful to students in the years ahead. The "green washing" of corporate agendas, in order to put profits on a "sustainable" basis, further undermines the awareness that we are on the cusp of life-changing events. And, if the rise of political extremism, patriotism, and the increasing craze for professional sports were not enough for envi-ronmental/cultural/educational reformers to overcome in getting their warnings to be taken seriously, there is now reactionary thinking that dominates governmental approaches to promoting educational reforms. The current effort to promote higher levels of educational achievement for all students is based on the same reductionist thinking in which the emphasis is on the measurement of learning outcomes. This orientation reduces education to learning isolated facts and events—which further strengthens the myth of the autonomous individual who is being pre-pared to succeed in college and in the workplace.

Unfortunately, the problem of cultural recursion is not limited to the reactionary educational-reform policies being pursued in the United States. The ten-year effort on the part of UNESCO, including the Guidelines and Recommendations Reorienting Teacher Education to

Address Sustainability—which has had world-wide exposure—promotes individual empowerment and the individual construction of knowledge as the primary means of achieving ecologically sustainable development (UNESCO, 2005). The sub-unit of UNESCO charged with promoting what in the literature is referred to as "ESD" (education for sustainable development) has established, throughout the world, regional networks of governmental organizations and cooperating colleges of education. Many of the recommendations for ESD reforms suggest the importance of taking local cultural traditions into account and preparing teachers for a world of continuing change. However, the process of recursive thinking is clearly evident in all the recommendations. With the exception of references to ESD, all the recommendations reflect the same level of generality, such as recommending "life-long learning" that can be found in earlier government documents that address educational reforms. Missing from the recommendations is any mention, even at the most general level, of the fundamental changes that must be introduced into teacher education that will lead to changes in consciousness and lifestyle.

The continual references to introducing reforms in teacher education that promote ESD may appear as praiseworthy, but the reality is that, unless there is greater specificity about the nature of the reforms that must be introduced, the map/territory problem identified by Gregory Bateson ensures that there will be little in the way of substantive change—except for greening of the rhetoric. The professors of education in different countries will simply reproduce the theoretical frameworks they learned in their years of graduate study—that is, their understanding of ESD will reflect the same silences that were part of their graduate studies 10 to 30 years ago when there was little awareness of the environmental crisis. The theories of John Dewey, who was a Social Darwinian and ethnocentric thinker, along with the critical pedagogy theorists, who promote critical inquiry without recognizing that it is based on many of the same deep cultural assumptions shared by the promoters of the industrial/consumer-dependent lifestyle, can easily be "green washed" by adopting key metaphors, such as "sustainability" and "sustainable development." But their conceptual maps, to stay with Bateson's metaphor, do not take into account the linguistic differences between cultures. Nor do they focus attention on what can be learned from cultures that have already developed ecological intelligence. They also ignore the nature of the culturally diverse cultural commons and the forces of enclosure, the linguistic colonization of the present by the past, and the linguistic colonization of other cultures.

The emphasis during the last 50 or so years on the individual empowerment now being promoted world-wide by the UNESCO project fails to address that critical inquiry must also be used to identify what needs to be conserved. Unless educational reforms that contribute to ESD are based on a radical rethinking of the taken-for-granted assumptions of previous generations, the rhetoric of ESD will continue to be an obstacle to moving to Level III thinking and to the ability to exercise ecological intelligence. As an educator attending a workshop in Switzerland on the conceptual underpinnings of ecologically intelligence complained: "What you are presenting to us about educational reforms that address the language, cultural commons, and ecological intelligence issues completely turns my thinking upside-down." She was recognizing that the educational reforms that address these issues could not be reconciled with UNESCO's agenda of promoting the individual construction of knowledge.

The problem is that these issues cannot be learned in sufficient depth in a short lecture or evening a two or three day workshop. There are too many layers of assumptions and taken-for-granted practices based on the ecology of good intentions and the misconceptions inherited from earlier generations. This problem is magnified by the current habit of assuming that complex ideas and reforms can be understood by reading a single article or, at most, a book that presents a radical challenge to current orthodoxies. The problems of recursive thinking, short attention spans, and the willingness to settle for a surface understanding of complex issues need to be taken into account when suggesting reforms that promote the widespread exercise of ecological intelligence. Thus, the challenge is to identify the key concepts that will enable teacher educators and university professors to recognize whether they are reinforcing individual or ecological intelligence. When the key concepts that clarify the differences between individual and ecological intelligence are recognized, it will be easier to understand how current misconceptions and silences perpetuated by the dominant languaging processes reinforce the myth of individual intelligence.

Fritjof Capra's description of systems thinking is a good starting place for assessing which pathway educational reforms are taking us down—pathways that should be recognized by the elementary-school teacher as well as by the graduate-level university professor. Capra's description of the characteristics of systems thinking is what has been referred to here as the exercise of ecological intelligence—though I would suggest several additions to his explanation. What Bateson calls an elementary idea or bit of information, that is, the difference which makes a difference, is always a part of what Capra identifies as "systems thinking," which includes the *pattern of organization*, a *structure* that embodies that system's pattern of organization, and a life-sustaining *process*. A summary of his explanation of these three components of living systems is as follows:

> The *pattern of organization* of any system, living or nonliving, is the configuration of relationships among the system's components that determine the system's essential characteristics. In other words, certain relationships must be present for something to be recognized as—say—a chair, a bicycle, or a tree.
>
> The *structure* of a system is the physical embodiment of its pattern of organization.... The description of the structure involves describing the system's physical components—their shape, chemical composition, and so forth.
>
> To find out whether a particular system—a crystal, a virus, a cell, or the planet Earth—is alive (that is, a life *process*), all we need to do is to find out whether its pattern of organization is that of an autopoietic network.... Autopoiesis (a concept borrowed from Humberto Maturana and Francisco Varela), or "self-making," is a network pattern in which the function of each component is to participate in the production or transformation of other components in the network. In this way the network continually makes itself. (1996, pp. 160–163)

What Bateson refers to as the ecology of differences (information circulating through the cultural and natural systems), which he also refers to as the ecology of Mind, always involves networks of relationships and patterns that interconnect. Isolating and abstracting any part as though it were a complete unit or thing is to impose an old pattern of thinking that leads to a distorted understanding.

I prefer the phrase "ecological intelligence" over the phrase "systems thinking" as the metaphor "systems" is too easily associated with the mechanical world of interacting parts. Capra avoids making this association by explaining its relevance for understanding biological phenomena. He also acknowledges the importance of Bateson's ideas. Nevertheless, my preference for using ecological intelligence is that it aligns more easily with other core ideas of Bateson's thinking that relate directly to understanding biological phenomena; namely, that ecologies—whether cultural or natural—have a history, and that the inability to recognize differences that sustain living systems may be rooted in the role that language plays in carrying forward what will be recognized and ignored, and how it will be interpreted. Another basic difference is that the phrase "systems thinking," unlike the phrase "ecological intelligence," does not suggest the need to engage in Level III thinking where the culture's deep taken-for-granted assumptions need to be questioned in terms of whether they contribute to living within the limits and possibilities of the earth's ecosystems.

Ecological intelligence also has other characteristics. These include an emphasis on understanding the history and diversity of cultural influences on events. The focus may be on the emergence of a particular cultural approach to creativity, science, technology, dealing with territorial boundaries, how individuality is expressed, the way traditions are understood, and so forth. Just as there is no force of nature called "progress" in Capra's understanding of systems thinking, there is no force of nature that ensures that change inherently leads to progress. Exercising ecological intelligence would focus on the history of cultural forces that have led to a taken-for-granted pattern of thinking. This is where educating students to exercise ecological intelligence would emphasize the importance of examining the recursive patterns of thinking, which might lead to examining the guiding mythopoetic narratives—including the modern ones that contribute to hiding the cultural impacts of technological innovations.

Exercising ecological intelligence requires giving constant attention to economic and religious forces, as well as to the different forms of power exercised by elite groups—which, in turn, would lead to examining their strategies for maintaining power and privileges. The role that metaphorical language plays in maintaining relationships of power would also be the focus of ecological intelligence. For example, what are the connections between the study of such high-status forms of knowledge as the ideas of Plato and other western abstract thinkers and the inability of students of these elite thinkers to recognize that there is an ecological crisis—and that its earliest sources of influence can be traced to such thinkers as John Locke, Adam Smith, René Descartes, and even

John Dewey? How has language helped to sustain patterns of inequality? These questions and others, such as why our political leaders persist in pursuing policies that are intended to introduce individualism, democracy, and free markets into cultures based on entirely different assumptions, would lead to examining a wide variety of conceptual antecedents and economic forces.

Overall, the dominant question, which has changed at different periods in western history, has now become: Do the relationships, as well as the patterns of thinking that guide daily behaviors and national policies, impact the natural ecologies in ways that promote life—or do they, given the current level of addiction to consumerism and the number of synthetic chemicals introduced into the environment and our bodies, alter, in fundamental ways, the ability of different systems to reproduce themselves and thus to keep alive the food webs of life?

The discussion of making the transition from individual to ecological intelligence a major focus of educational reform that extends from the early grades through graduate school may appear to be too theoretical and thus beyond the interest of public school teachers. This would be unfortunate as public school teachers exert a powerful influence on the process of cultural reproduction—particularly by passing on many of the culture's basic assumptions that are seldom examined in the later grades. These assumptions include equating change (especially technologically based changes) with progress, thinking of traditions as sources of backwardness and language as a conduit in a sender/receiver process of communication, and the importance of elevating self-interest above all other values—which is often expressed as "learning to be authentic." The alchemy of the elementary classroom—indeed, of most grades extending through middle school—includes a genuine concern for the well-being of the students, an overwhelming number of explanations that get reduced to isolated facts and events, reified deep cultural assumptions, the teacher's abdication to the magic of computer-mediated learning and the mind-set of the people who write the educational software programs, and elements of the teacher's ideological and religious beliefs that frame the explanations that become part of the curriculum.

The explanations of different aspects of culture that students encounter in classrooms for the first time are likely to have a lasting influence on the student's taken-for-granted interpretative framework. Examples of how many adults fail to question explanations that are learned during their most vulnerable, and thus most dependent, phase of development can be seen in how they reproduce the same explanations that become part of the socialization of the next generation. Textbook examples include how students should understand the nature of the brain (now often explained as like a computer), what constitutes a human resource that can be used to one's own benefit (family and friends, according to one textbook), how to think about technology (as a neutral tool), the settlement of the West by pioneers (as though it were not already settled), and so forth. As many classroom teachers and university professors do not question the assumptions that underlie the explanations that are part of the students' earliest period of socialization to the culture's basic patterns of thinking, the underlying assumptions are too often taken for granted over the students' lifetime. The silences that are part of this process of primary socialization, which are part of the initial interpretative frameworks of the dominant culture, are also influenced by the mis-education teachers receive in their professional courses and from faculty in other disciplines. Like the alchemy of earlier times, this approach to education does not lead to people being able to exercise ecological intelligence—which today would be the equivalent of gold. Instead, it is leading to a form of individualism that thinks in slogans, has no accurate knowledge of the culture's own history or the history of other cultures and has little interest in considering which forms of self-limitation are necessary for conserving the natural systems upon which future generations will rely. The dominant ethos is summed up in the Nike slogan, "Just Do It."

Given the current "race to the top" approach to educational reform being sponsored by the federal and state governments, and given the late twentieth-century mind-set that still dominates in most colleges of education and in the social sciences and humanities, it would be easy to think that the scale of resistance is too great to warrant the effort of promoting the exercise of ecological intelligence. Yet, the early feminist, civil rights, and labor activists also faced what seemed to be overwhelming opposition to the need to make fundamental changes. If Bateson's important insight—which is that humans are not independent observers and manipulators of natural system, but are participants in the information networks that make up the larger ecological system—is ignored, it is likely that the explanation of systems thinking, or even of ecological intelligence, will become just one more theory among a host of others that can be more easily marketed.

Granted, making the exercise of ecological intelligence part of the individual's embodied experience will be difficult in a culture in which the dominant assumptions are centered on viewing the individual as the source of rationality, democratic decision-making, consumer spending, seeking happiness and personal success, being a candidate for being raptured-up into a heaven of eternal bliss, and so forth. Yet, this is exactly the reform that needs to be undertaken. Exercising ecological intelligence needs to become part of the students' culturally mediated embodied experiences—which will engage all the physical senses, along with memory and a heightened aesthetic awareness and moral responsibility. It cannot be experienced as a procedure that is followed only in certain situations, such as learning to exercise ecological intelligence in a biology class and then reverting back to the old pattern of exercising individual intelligence in other classes and in society.

As suggested earlier, we already rely upon ecological intelligence when it is recognized that undesirable consequences will follow if close attention is not given to all the messages (differences) circulating through the context of which one is a part. Just as in Bateson's example of how the person swinging an ax adjusts each stroke in a way that takes account of the difference caused by the previous stroke, the exercise of ecological intelligence involves being fully aware of the different information networks—including being aware that cutting the tree may disrupt the habitat that is relied upon by other members of the larger food web. Learning the patterns of interdependencies and thinking in terms of relationships and continuities in both cultural and natural ecologies is important, as they provide the necessary conceptual frameworks for recognizing both how past misconceptions and practices have put the culture on the pathway of ecologically destructive practices, as well as how current behaviors are likely to impact the future. This form of learning will have profoundly different consequences from that when behaviors and values are based on cultural assumptions about a human-centered world, where the natural systems can be thought of in terms of mechanistic processes, and science and technology will find ways to overcome changes in the natural systems that are limiting economic growth, and so forth. It's not that the exercise of ecological intelligence requires excluding all previous forms of learning. Rather, learning the history of ideas, social theories, forces of domination and social injustice, forms of addiction and their connections with the dominant economic system, etc., is essential to recognizing the misconceptions that have put us on such an ecologically unsustainable path. This background knowledge is essential to being able to recognize which relationships and patterns need to be affirmed, and thus supported, as part of an eco-justice-oriented democracy.

The important question is not whether the exercise of ecological intelligence is more effective when the individual has been freed of prior conceptual influences—as Paulo Freire and his followers suggest when claiming that socialization represents a banking approach to learning and thus can be replaced by relying entirely upon critical reflection (1971, p. 31). This view of emancipating the student from past influences is echoed in the widespread claim that students should construct their own knowledge. The critical question is: Does what the student learns make it more difficult to exercise ecological intelligence in deciding social policies, in assessing the impacts of new technologies, in recognizing when other cultures have taken a more ecologically sustainable approach to development? Several examples might help clarify how to change the traditional approaches to learning that have marginalized awareness of the cultural roots of the ecological crisis. In the following examples, the traditional content of the discipline is not thrown out but is examined from an ecologically and culturally informed perspective.

The study of western philosophers is generally held up as essential to being well educated. Yet, it is important to consider whether learning about the ideas of these philosophers leaves students with a number of conceptual barriers to being able to recognize that ideas exist within a larger ecological network of information exchanges and interdependencies. The approach that characterizes most departments of philosophy is to read the arguments made by various philosophers—ranging from the pre-Socratics, Plato, on down to Dewey—on the nature of reality and what constitutes knowledge, on the basis of moral judgment, on the basis of mind/body separation, on the universal connections between free inquiry and social progress. What is distinctive about this approach, and how it has contributed to many of the ecological and political problems we now face, is that it helped to create a class of elite thinkers who were conditioned to think in abstractions and to impose their abstractions— that is, the supposedly universal truths about property rights, individualism, free markets, what constitutes knowledge, and so forth—on other cultures as well as their own. Students of western philosophy were, and still are, largely unaware of the ethnocentrism of the philosophers they study. Other silences of the major philosophers exclude any discussion of the importance of the cultural and environmental commons and what Shiva calls Earth Democracy. The effect of this legacy can be seen in how the few philosophy courses that now address environmental issues are largely oriented to introducing students to the writings of environmentalists, such as Aldo Leopold, Wendell Berry, and ecofeminists. Unfortunately, these writers fail to provide the knowledge and skills necessary for living less toxic and less consumer-dependent lives. But still, this limited exposure does raise consciousness—even to the point of being receptive to a more explicit awareness of exercising ecological intelligence.

The earlier question about the forms of general background knowledge that provide an historical framework for guiding the exercise of ecological intelligence could be answered by taking an entirely different approach to the study of western philosophers, or to other areas of study, such as psychology, sociology, political science, religion, business, education, and so forth. Alternative approaches involve a process of reframing —that is, approaching what is being studied with a new set of questions.

Reframing how to study the ideas of Plato, Aristotle, Hobbes, Locke, Smith, Rousseau, Bentham, Mill, Hegel, Marx, Spencer, Dewey, and others in the pantheon of influential thinkers would involve examining how their abstract theories fail to take account of the local cultural practices relating to the cultural and environmental commons, and the differences in cultural ways of knowing. Questioning the silences and deeply held cultural assumptions, particularly how they influence understanding the nature of science and technology, as well as how the prescriptive aspects of the philosophers' theories would impact the patterns of mutual support in local communities and natural systems, would also be part of this reframing process. For example, one of the most fundamental ecologically and community disrupting forces can be traced to the thinking of such philosophers as Locke and Smith whose abstract (that is, culturally uninformed) theories about the universal nature of private property and free markets helped to frame how another aspect of individual autonomy is to be understood; namely, as being free of any moral responsibility for exploiting the environment and other people. This view of individualism, which has recently been extended to corporations, grants the right to establish private ownership over nearly every aspect of daily life that previously was shared and renewed largely outside of a money economy. This process of enclosure also extends to incorporating all aspects of the natural commons (air, water, forests, soil, plants, animals, genes, etc.) into the free-market system in which private ownership and monetization contribute to the spread of poverty and to the rapid exploitation of the environment.

Nearly every discipline in universities could be transformed if its traditions were examined in terms of how the diversity of the world's local cultural and natural commons were undermined by the religious, ideological, economic, and other sources of abstract thinking that can be traced to earlier philosophers, political theorists, and theologians. How was the distinction established, in different historical periods, between what constituted high and low-status knowledge? What traditions of self-sufficiency were lost when new forms of knowledge and elites emerged and became widely accepted? To what extent was colonization a result of the degraded environments of the colonizing powers—and what were the forces responsible for exploiting the environment? What were the forces, at different times in western history, that led to undermining the wide range of artisans and craftspeople, and transforming the creative arts from being part of community life into categories of low and high status? Was the commodification of an art essential to it being accorded high status? How has the metaphorical language of different cultural groups, in different periods of western history, undermined the local practice of ecological intelligence that has been refined over generations of place-based observation and experience?

Given what scientists are reporting on the rapid rate of changes in the earth's natural systems, and given the pressures of the current population—which has expanded from just over one billion at the turn of the twentieth century to close to seven billion today—we don't have the centuries it took the feminist, civil rights, and labor activists to achieve their goals of social justice. At most, we may have a generation or two to make the transition to more sustainable patterns of living. Given this possibility, it is necessary for faculty to begin asking whether their fields of inquiry and courses would be more useful to the upcoming generations if they were reframed by focusing on the traditions of unsustainable and sustainable cultural developments.

There is a consensus among scientists that climate change is

occurring and that it results from human activity. And, there is a growing understanding that minor changes in temperature have fundamental
consequences for biological and weather systems. While our industrial
system of production and consumption, along with the media, sustain
the false picture of the crisis as a short-term phenomenon to be overcome
by advances in technology, scientists are warning that the time-frame
for making fundamental changes in cultural practices may be as short
as two or three generations. This means that by the time the students
now in the early grades become teachers, professors, politicians, economists, and media experts, they will need to be prepared to communicate
in a vocabulary that is not based on the analogs settled upon by the
earlier thinkers who laid the conceptual and moral foundations for the
industrial/consumer-oriented culture that, with the aid of science and
technology, promised endless progress. They will also need an education
that will enable them to promote practices, technologies, and policies
that contribute to revitalizing the cultural commons and protecting the
environmental commons—both of which are being undermined by the
economic, ideological, and religious forces based on the abstractions of
earlier eras. If the generation now sitting in classrooms, participating in
computer-mediated social networking, and addicted to various forms
of self-indulgence, ranging from eating junk food to buying the latest
peer-group-approved consumer item, is unable to get the message across
to the following generation, there will be little hope for the future of
humanity. In effect, if the educational process remains as ineffective
as it is today in promoting ecologically sustainable communities and
lifestyles, the scholarly achievements of past and of current university
faculty will be viewed as entirely irrelevant—much as the ruins of previous civilizations. That is, if the search for food, shelter, and safety even
allows the environmental refugees to consider them.

Practical Steps to Making the Exercise of Ecological Intelligence Part of Students' Taken-for-Granted Experience

Exercising ecological intelligence occurs naturally in many contexts in
which we are fully present in the sense of being aware of the information (differences) being communicated by the other natural and human
participants, including adapting our responses to what is being communicated in response to our actions. Unlike the Cartesian individual, who
is an outsider acting on an unintelligent world, or the Other (in Martin

Buber's sense), who is an object we manipulate, exercising ecological intelligence involves a collaborative process. To recall how Bateson puts it, "The total self-correcting unit which processes information, or, as I say, 'thinks' and 'acts' and 'decides,' is a *system* whose boundaries do not at all coincide with the boundaries, either of the body or what is popularly called the 'self' or 'consciousness'; and it is important to notice that there are *multiple* differences between the thinking system and the 'self' as popularly conceived" (1972, p. 319).

Of course, we can never entirely eliminate cultural influences—from our interpretations, from our short and long-term expectations, or from how our self-concept is influenced by ongoing interactions. As suggested earlier, many indigenous cultures provide explanatory frameworks that recognize the exercise of ecological intelligence as a normal aspect of daily life. In some instances, this is achieved through a shared belief system that does not represent the natural environment as a source of danger or as being wild and thus in need of control. Rather, in many indigenous cultures the interactions that are part of the collaborative exercising of ecological intelligence are understood as a source of knowledge essential to sustaining the life of the community while not also destroying the sources of life in the earth community.

The explanatory frameworks of the West, especially those influenced by western philosophers and theorists who established the tradition of viewing the everyday world of experience as always falling short of the perfections stipulated in their abstract theories, have been carried forward in the metaphorically layered languaging processes that construct the "reality" of the new members born into the language community. Under the guidance of theologians and philosophers, the idea that the peasant was unintelligent, and thus could not be educated, was largely taken for granted. The idea that there are many different forms and levels of intelligence operating in the natural systems—from the behavior of genes to the interdependencies of plants and animals—was and still is beyond what these philosophers could understand. With the acceptance of the earliest western cultural formulations of the idea that the individual is the basic social unit—as having a soul and a destiny dependent upon living according to certain moral norms, as having the potential of influencing political outcomes, as being free of all traditional forms of knowledge, as existing as an objective and rational observer of an external mechanistic world that needs to be brought under rational control—the West moved onto a destructive ecological trajectory.

In effect, the tradition of individuals who experience the world as something separate and exploitable, and thus who are unaccountable for what they introduce into the environment in the name of scientific and material progress, is learned. This self-centered individual has no genetic basis other than the capacity to learn to think and communicate in highly symbolic languages. And, as Edward Sapir, Benjamin Lee Whorf, Peter Berger, and Thomas Luckmann have argued, the languaging processes of a culture intergenerationally construct what is taken to be "reality" within the culture. The experience of being an independent observer of an external world, as well as all the assumptions about human/nature relationships and possibilities, are cultural constructions. Just as recent reinterpretations of what is "real" and "normal" have occurred in the area of social justice, youth can be socialized to experience as "real" and "normal" a different relationship with the cultural and natural ecologies. That is, the process of socialization (education) can be altered through exposure to different narratives (which are now beginning to take place in children's literature) and to different vocabularies where the metaphors are framed by analogs that highlight the patterns and relationships that connect rather than the analogs that suggest separation and the need to control.

It is quite possible, indeed likely, that Capra's explanation of systems thinking will be interpreted by others as a strategy for more effectively exercising control over the natural systems. That is, the Cartesian form of individualism is not incompatible with systems thinking—especially if the individual still takes for granted the main cultural assumptions about the nature of progress, rationality, and a human-centered world. This possibility brings into focus the challenge that confronts classroom teachers and university professors who are engaged in expanding the linguistic foundations of what will be experienced and interpreted as "reality." There are many educational contexts in which a critical distinction reinforces how the individual will understand her/his relationships to, or within, the larger system. The distinction may be in the difference between when a student is asked to project onto the Other what she/he has previously learned as the culturally sanctioned answer or explanation, and when the student is encouraged to give attention to the patterns that connect—and to the autopoietic networks within which she/he is a participant (including the consequences of the student's action that flow outward and affect other participants in the system). Both explanations are "reality" constructing experiences, and the classroom teacher and university professor play a powerful mediating role—especially when the same cultural patterns are reinforced by others. Hopefully, the patterns will lead to the ongoing realization that all interactions within the cultural and natural ecologies require giving closer attention to the information exchanges flowing through the systems, and to whether the individual's actions strengthen or weaken the viability of the systems as a whole. In short, one of the primary educational objectives is to replace the current taken-for-granted attitude of being an autonomous individual who has a privileged perspective on an external world that can be manipulated or ignored, depending upon the immediate interests of the student.

One of the most fundamental misconceptions that needs to be overcome is that the individual's own subjective understanding of the ecological crisis is all that matters. This misconception underlies the individual's self-proclaimed right and responsibility to decide whether climate change is occurring, and, if so, if it is attributable to human behavior or is part of the earth's historical cycles of warming and cooling. This populist way of thinking now combines with a friend/enemy approach to political discourse that makes it exceedingly difficult to reach agreement on such issues as the multiple dangers of hyper-consumerism, the excessive reliance upon synthetic chemicals, and the exploitation of aquifers and fish stocks—to cite just a few of our mounting environmental difficulties. Nevertheless, the current failure to agree that there is an ecological crisis, and that it has implications for what is being taught in our public schools and universities, does not mean the crisis will disappear.

Educators at all levels need to begin to introduce reforms that strengthen community self-reliance—which most left and right-wing political activists would have trouble arguing against. One result of community self-reliance is that it reduces dependence upon consumerism and the addiction to wanting the latest prescription drugs and mechanical technologies. This is likely to be seen as "un-American" by the market liberals who misrepresent themselves as conservatives. But most communities are not monolithic in terms of guiding their mytho-poetic narratives, and an increasing number of religious groups are beginning to think about their responsibilities as stewards of God's earthly creation. People already engaged in cultural commons activities wow!

will also be supportive of educational reforms that reduce the current unsustainable cycle of work-consumerism-increasing debt and drug dependency in which many Americans are trapped. Other aspects of the curricular reforms suggested here will be supported by advocates of social justice, particularly after they realize that the middle-class interpretation of social justice being promoted by many educational reformers does not take account of how overshooting the sustaining capacity of the natural systems will have the greatest impact on the poor and marginalized.

Many teachers expect specific lesson plans on how ecological intelligence can be reinforced in different curriculum units and experiences. True :) That is, the desire to know "how to do it" is too often the central focus of classroom teachers who feel overwhelmed by the many pressures with which they must deal. However, the social contexts and the students' cultural background, level of experience, and intellectual maturity are key elements in deciding how to frame the students' encounter with environmental and cultural issues. Presenting teachers with actual curriculum units contradicts the primary characteristics of ecological intelligence—and how to foster it. Rather than reinforcing the tendency to rely upon packaged learning experiences, the emphasis should be placed upon the teacher's awareness of the issues, misunderstandings being perpetuated by the curriculum, and examples of ecological thinking that can be introduced in different learning settings. Listed below is a summary of the main issues and concepts that can be brought into the discussion at almost any level of the educational process, and in almost every area of the curriculum. If the summary of ideas does not relate directly to helping students understand the differences between individual and ecological intelligence, it relates to reform issues connected with revitalizing the local cultural commons and to recognizing the different forms of enclosure. Learning about the local cultural commons and becoming actively involved in mentoring relationships is perhaps the most direct and effective way of learning to exercise ecological intelligence. Understanding the ideas and issues listed below should be part of the professional knowledge of every classroom teacher and university professor—regardless of specialized areas of teaching.

Easy, right?

Educational Reforms that Foster Ecological Intelligence

Ways in Which the Exercise of Ecological Intelligence is Undermined

1. Reinforcing the idea that the student should seek to be more autonomous—which occurs when students are encouraged to construct their own knowledge and values.
2. Reinforcing the pattern of thinking that describes plants, animals, people, events, data, and so forth, as independent entities.
3. Reinforcing the idea that change is inherently progressive in nature, and that critical thinking is the engine of change.
4. Reinforcing the idea that the individual is an independent thinker, observer, and source of action on an external environment (the Cartesian mind/body separation).
5. Reinforcing the ideas that traditions obstruct progress, that competition leads to the best ideas and plans of action, and that science and technology will solve all environmental problems.
6. Reinforcing the idea that words refer to real things and events—and can be universally generalized—and that there is such a thing as objective knowledge and data.
7. Reinforcing the current over-reliance on nouns that marginalize the awareness that the world is one of relationships and interdependencies.

Ways in Which the Exercise of Ecological Intelligence is Reinforced

1. Encouraging students to recognize that life-sustaining processes always involve relationships, including how ideas, values, events, behaviors, policy decisions, and so forth, are embedded in and influence interacting cultural and natural systems. The "difference which makes a difference," that Bateson says represents a basic unit of information, is another way of saying that relationships are an inescapable aspect of life-forming and life-sustaining processes. (The nature of the relationships may also be driven by what he refers to as "an ecology of life-destroying ideas and values.")
2. Encouraging students to recognize that the language they take for granted is part of a linguistic ecology—that words have a history and that the failure to recognize this may lead to relying upon the earlier ways of thinking that provided the conceptual basis for the

Industrial Revolution which has now entered the digital phase of globalization. There is also a need to encourage students to identify culturally and ecologically informed analogs that will reframe the meaning of words and thus the students' ability to consciously recognize the relationships that are ecologically sustainable, as well as those that are not.

3. Encouraging students to recognize how abstract thinking marginalizes the need to give attention to the immediate context—and to the patterns within the different cultural and natural systems.

4. Encouraging students to recognize that critical thinking has a role to play in the exercise of ecological intelligence, but that it should take account both of what needs to be intergenerationally renewed and what needs to be radically changed. Students should be encouraged to examine how a human-centered view of the role of critical thinking leads to critical thinking being used by corporations to bring more aspects of the natural systems and the cultural commons under the control of market forces.

5. Encouraging students to consider the differences between oral and print-based forms of cultural storage and communication—especially how those differences take account of the local cultural and natural systems.

6. Encouraging students to shift from thinking of themselves as autonomous actors and observers of an external social and environmental world to basing their self-identity on how their relationships contribute to the well-being of others in both the cultural and natural ecologies in which they are embedded.

7. Encouraging students to assess how their personal state of consciousness, including feelings of greed, anger, fear, the need to control, and the need to belong, marginalizes both their awareness of the ecology of relationships and patterns, as well as whether their responses are destructive—which, when reflected upon, may increase their personal anxieties. *true*

The Linguistic Colonization of the Present by the Past —and of Other Cultures

Students need to be introduced to two aspects of how the metaphorical nature of most of our words carries forward the misconceptions and *Agreed* silences of earlier thinkers who were unaware of environmental limits.

First, students need to learn how many of their patterns of thinking are based on a view of language that too many faculty take for granted; namely, a conduit view of language that is based on a sender/receiver model of communication. This leads to the idea that words refer to real things, that words have universal meanings, and that language is the means for communicating objective facts and information. Second, students need to be able to recognize the following if they are to become more critically aware of how they may be relying upon the same patterns of thinking that are now overshooting environmental limits.

1. Most words are metaphors.
2. The choice of analogs by earlier thinkers continues to frame the current meaning of words—such as freedom, individualism, progress, tradition, markets, and so forth.
3. Words (metaphors) have a history and thus may carry forward the misconceptions and silences of earlier thinkers who were influenced by the cultural assumptions of their era.
4. The interpretative frameworks that have organized social life over hundreds of years, influence behaviors and values, and marginalize awareness of aspects of experience, are based on root metaphors. Root metaphors, such as patriarchy, anthropocentrism, individualism, mechanism, progress, etc., illuminate certain ways of understanding while hiding other possibilities.
5. It is possible, indeed necessary in light of the ecological crisis, to reframe the meaning of much of the modernizing vocabulary by identifying analogs that are culturally and ecologically informed—words, such as progress, individualism, intelligence, community, technology, poverty, wealth, etc.
6. The analogs based on the culture's understanding of the attributes, and thus the meaning, of words such as woman, weed, wilderness, uncivilized, resource, and so forth, carry forward how moral behavior is governed by the cultural understanding of the attributes of the Other—person, plant, physical environment.
7. The conduit view of language, along with the idea that words stand for real things and thus have a universal meaning, are the academic version of the Trojan horse that is part of the process of colonizing other cultures. This process of linguistic colonization, along with the economic and technological forces of colonization, undermine

the intergenerational knowledge, developed over generations, of how to live more community-centered and less environmentally destructive lives.

Educational Reforms that Contribute to Revitalizing the Local Cultural Commons and to an Understanding of the Modern Forms of Enclosure

Many of the metaphors we rely upon today, and whose meanings were framed both by analogs chosen in the distant past and by current evocative experiences (such as experiences with different technologies or world-shaping events), continue to marginalize an awareness of the ecological importance of the local cultural commons—as well as the diversity of the world's cultural commons. The following represents a highly simplified overview of key concepts and issues.

1. The cultural commons are largely the intergenerational knowledge, skills, and mentoring relationships that exist in every community— and are less dependent upon consumerism and a money economy.
2. The cultural commons vary from community to community according to the traditions of the community's ethnic groups and bioregions.
3. The cultural commons include the knowledge, practices, and inter-generational processes of sharing and renewal in the areas of food, healing, ceremonies, narratives, languages, the creative arts, craft knowledge and skills, games, volunteering and community activism, civil liberties and social justice movements, and so forth.
4. The networks of relationships and mentoring in each of these areas have a smaller carbon and toxic footprint—as they involve face-to-face relationships and local systems of economic exchange.
5. In an era of downsizing, automation, and outsourcing, the cultural commons provide ways in which people can discover their talents, interests, and experience of community while becoming less dependent upon a money economy.
6. Not all expressions of the cultural commons meet the current standards of social justice and ecologically responsible citizenship—thus, the cultural commons should not be romanticized.

The Pedagogical and Curricular Implications of Introducing Students to the Local Cultural Commons

1. Introducing the cultural commons must include descriptions of the various local activities, how they are culturally diverse, and how they are being enclosed—which can lead to an in-depth analysis of the modern forces that are market-oriented and driven by misconceptions and silences in the educational process.

2. The students' introduction to the cultural commons should be experience based—where they are encouraged to describe their own cultural commons experiences, as well as engage in surveys of the other largely non-monetized activities and relationships in their community. Participating in these groups will lead to mentoring relationships that will contribute to students acquiring many of the competencies essential to an ecologically sustainable future.

3. The students' description of experiences in the local cultural commons should take the form of a phenomenological description of their embodied experiences rather than relying upon textbooks and other forms of print-based descriptions. Students should identify their mentors, give attention to the complexity and interdependency of social networks, as well as make explicit their experience of community when involved in the different cultural commons activities.

4. Helping students become explicitly aware of the differences in their embodied experiences (including discovering interests, developing talents, participating in community-supportive relationships), as they move between engagement in some area of the cultural commons and a monetized and industrialized setting, is essential to their acquiring the language necessary for exercising the communicative competence to resist further forms of enclosure of the cultural and environmental commons.

5. Teachers need to understand their mediating role in helping students to become explicitly aware of the differences between their experiences in the cultural commons and in monetized relationships. This involves being aware of what questions to ask in order to help students become aware of what they might otherwise take for granted. Prescribing what the students should think should be avoided. Instead, the teacher's mediating role is to encourage the examination of the relationships and ecological impacts—which

may lead students to recognizing aspects of the scientific/industrial culture that are making positive contributions to humankind and to living more ecologically sustainable lives.

6. Creating close alliances with groups engaged in sustaining different aspects of the cultural commons will help to provide mentoring relationships that will contribute to the students' competencies—especially the competencies that are community and environmentally enhancing.

7. Teachers need to acquire a balanced way of thinking about how to ensure that the students' understanding of the tensions between the cultural commons and the market-driven economy, and other sources of enclosure, does not become ideologically driven. The students need to develop the ability to think critically about how technologies and other aspects of the industrial/monetized culture influence the cultural commons, and how the cultural commons can be promoted as alternatives to the ecologically destructive impacts of the market-liberal globalizing forces. That is, students need to learn that they stand at an important ecological juncture where knowing what to conserve is as important as knowing what needs to be reformed or abandoned entirely.

Understanding the Cultural Transforming Characteristics of Computer-Mediated Learning and Communicating

Computer-mediated thinking and communication reinforce the conduit (the sender/receiver) view of language. Thus, computer-mediated thinking makes it difficult to recognize that words are metaphors and that they have a history rooted in specific cultural ways of thinking that can be traced to the past. The current idea being promoted in some countries is that students should use computers as the primary resource for constructing their own knowledge. This approach to educational reform ignores that the culture/metaphor/thought connections are hidden by the conduit view of language that computers reinforce.

1. The educational uses of computers, as well as uses in other settings, involve the encounter of the user (e.g., the student) with the interpretative framework and value system of the people who wrote the program. The student is not encountering an objective representation of some aspect of "reality."

2. Only explicit forms of knowledge can be digitized—and those will reflect the interpretive framework of the observer. That is, the aspects of cultural experience that are taken for granted, as well as the tacit understandings and the lived context of human-with-human relationships, and human relationships with the natural environment, cannot be digitized. Even videos of experiences are unable to represent personal memory, taken-for-granted patterns of thinking, and other internal states of consciousness. In a twist on the Cartesian mind/body separation, the visual and audio dimensions of experience that can be digitized are limited to the aspects of embodied experience that are accessible to the outside observer, which will be influenced, in turn, by the assumptions that the observer brings to the relationship. What the outside observer cannot digitize are the internal states of consciousness—including the Other's experience of self-identity.

3. Computer-mediated learning and communication carry forward the gains and losses associated with the tradition of print-based storage and communication. Like other uses of print, computers reinforce the abstract thinking and communication which easily lead to assuming that print-based representations of reality can be generalized across cultures.

4. Educational software programs are based on the taken-for-granted patterns of thinking of the people who create them—and often reinforce the assumptions that further impede the process of relational thinking that is an aspect of ecological intelligence.

5. There are many ways in which computers can be used to map green spaces, represent energy and toxic flows in the environment, and connect members of the community who are engaged in sustaining the local cultural commons.

6. Teacher education programs need to introduce future teachers to the culture-mediating characteristics of computers. This should lead, in turn, to introducing students to the questions they should ask about the cultural assumptions being reinforced in software programs, as well as to considering how the increased reliance upon computers leads to greater dependence upon the money economy, increased demand on sources of energy, and increased exposure to the toxic chemicals when the computers are discarded.

Learning to Exercise Ecological Intelligence

If classroom teachers and university professors do not learn to think in terms of the interconnected world of the cultural and natural systems, it will be exceedingly difficult for them to reinforce this way of thinking among students. The tendency will be to perpetuate the old patterns that make the individual the center of political, moral, and lifestyle decisions. It is for this reason that educators at all levels need to become better informed about the changes occurring in the chemistry of the world's oceans, the synthetic chemicals that are altering the reproductive capacity of humans and other members of the biotic community, the changes in weather patterns that are melting glaciers and releasing greenhouse gases into the atmosphere, the expansion of deserts and the loss of topsoil—and the number of people who are becoming environmental refugees as a result of these and other environmental changes. If classroom teachers and university professors do not keep these environmental changes foremost in mind, the tendency will be to reinforce the patterns of thinking and values that have been major contributors to the ecologically unsustainable, modern, western approach to progress. That this approach to progress is now being globalized in a world of nearly seven billion people means that the crisis will deepen at an accelerating rate—and, as the crisis deepens, the politics of national and individual self-interest will lead to increased conflicts that will, in turn, further marginalize constructive approaches to addressing how to mitigate both human suffering and the further destruction of the natural systems.

This scenario does not have to occur. There are many cultures, especially in the Third World, that are working to recover their traditions of community self-sufficiency and environmental stewardship. There are also many cultures in which the dominant religious/cultural practices do not equate progress and well-being with the accumulation of material wealth and the exploitation of other people and the environment. And, in many communities in the West there are people whose lives are focused on participating in community-building cultural commons activities. Thus, as suggested earlier, there is no need for intellectuals to create an abstract model of how people should learn to live within socially just and ecologically sustainable communities. However, it is important to note that the people practicing ecological intelligence are a distinct minority and, perhaps more importantly, they do not occupy positions of power within corporations, in the dominant political

✳ Unfortunately true!
Change will be very hard!

establishments, or in the military.

The challenge for educators is to help ensure that the next generation will be educated in ways that make them receptive to learning from
other cultures as well as the community/cultural commons-centered
groups in their own culture. This is essential if the cycle of mentoring
one generation by the next is to continue. How to encourage faculty
to take these issues seriously, and to avoid hiding behind the tradition
of academic freedom that justifies ignoring the ecological crisis on the
grounds that one's chosen scholarly field of inquiry takes priority over all
else, is a problem that is not amenable to a technological fix—just as the
moments of awakening that lead to a transformed state of consciousness
cannot be forced.

While keeping the above problems in mind, it is important to return
to the question of how classroom teachers and university professors can
use this list of issues and ideas to reinforce the students' ability to think
and act in ecologically responsible ways. Given the four areas in which all
teachers/professors make critically important decisions—in the areas of
linguistic colonization, cultural/environmental commons lifestyle issues,
the differences between oral and technologically mediated communication and thinking, and the exercise of individual or ecological intelligence—there is little in the way of existing courses that provide textbook
answers to the questions that might come up in classroom discussions—
or in PowerPoint presentations. If, as Bateson, Capra, Maturana, and
Varela point out, ecological thinking involves observing and adapting
one's responses to the differences which make a difference—that is, the
patterns that connect within and between different systems (including
the cultural and biological systems)—then, when the teacher/professor
asks a question about how the analogs settled upon in the distant past
influence current thinking as well as what is being ignored, answers will
emerge from an examination of the myriad cultural patterns of the past,
the earlier cultural assumptions, the cultural approaches to the natural
systems, and so forth. The learning process will require examining the
relationships, patterns, and impacts that connect the past to the present.
It will also bring into focus the moral values and democratic decision-
making that reinforce different patterns and relationships. The question
about the history of words can be raised in a very preliminary way in the
early grades and explored in much greater depth at the graduate level. At
both levels a key idea is being introduced that, hopefully, will stay with

the student into adulthood; namely, that words have a history and carry forward ways of thinking that may be ecologically problematic.

To cite another example, asking students about the differences between their experience in some activity of the cultural commons and their experience in a consumer relationship leads to an examination of the patterns that connect—perhaps between the guiding economic ideology and the behaviors and values that the students should pursue if they are to have a positive self-image. The patterns that connect might lead to exploring the differences between learning a skill and discovering a talent that leads to mentoring relationships with others, and being a consumer that leaves a toxic footprint. Questioning the deep cultural assumptions, asking questions about how the cultural and environmental commons are being privatized and monetized by the market system (such as the corporate ownership of human genes, etc.), and mapping what remains of the local cultural and environmental commons, all reinforce the exercise of ecological intelligence. It is possible to make the same case for all the other issues and ideas listed under the four categories of teacher/professor decision-making. Whether the focus is on questions relating to how computers reinforce abstract thinking, and thus individual intelligence (which is itself an important question to explore), or on considering the appropriate and inappropriate uses of communication technologies as they relate to sustainable cultural and natural systems, the field of inquiry is as wide-open as the complexity of the cultural and natural ecologies. In these and other examples that can easily be cited from the above list, the outcome should not a list of facts and objective knowledge that is to be memorized and reproduced on a test required by the bureaucrats' "race-to-the-top" governmental policy.

Educational reforms need to make a genuine break from the industrial approach to public education and from the academic imperialism that is at the root of economic and technological globalization. Adapting pedagogical and curricular decisions to what is required by packaged curriculum units and measurable test scores may appear as freeing the teacher from the task of identifying the boundaries and focus of a curriculum that will engage the interest of students, but it becomes *true* repetitive and personally unfulfilling after a few years—just as working on the assembly line that encodes the intelligence and assumptions of the experts who designed the system becomes repetitive. The industrial approach to public education and, to a lesser extent, a university education does not prepare students for democratic decision-making in the cultural and natural ecological systems, or for clarifying the ecologically sustainable values that represent alternatives to the individually centered industrial culture that is the source of increasing poverty and environmental destruction. The ideas of Bateson provide the conceptual framework for judging whether the educational process is reinforcing an ecology of unsustainable ideas and values. Hopefully, others will begin to take seriously how his ideas help clarify the cultural roots of the ecological crisis, how the West's recursive conceptual traditions have contributed to the cultural colonization that is at the center of increasingly global-wide conflicts, and how to revitalize local economies, local decision-making, and approaches to education.

CHAPTER 8

Is a Systemic Education Transcending the 'I' Even Imaginable?
Some Reflections from German-Speaking Europe

By Rolf Jucker, Director,
Swiss Foundation for Environmental Education

> Atomization into fine paranoiac particles. Hysterization of contact. The more I want to be me, the more I feel an emptiness. The more I express myself, the more I am drained. The more I run after myself, the more tired I get. We cling to our self like a coveted job title. (The Invisible Committee, 2007)

For any observer who has no particular financial or other vested interests in the status quo, the following three statements are obvious and backed up with ample scientific evidence:

1. Planet Earth as a whole, various subsystems, such as climate change, the nitrogen cycle, economic interactions, societies, communities, and, of course, human "individuals," cannot be properly understood, except as layered, interactive, interdependent self-renewing sub-systems.

2. Starting with the Industrial Revolution, and with increasing speed and volume, human interference with various systems on various levels, but also with the underlying life-support system Planet Earth itself, has led to a situation where we are severely transgressing the safe operating space, i.e., planetary boundaries (Rockström, et al., 2009). This means that we need to resize human activity within these boundaries.

3. Taken together this implies that we need a radical, epistemological shift that affects all levels of interaction (including our underlying thinking and understanding, i.e., our use of language and mental models). In other words: We need to abandon our reductionist,

rational, Cartesian world-view for a systemic one which is characterized by Bateson's ecological intelligence as elaborated in previous chapters.

The trouble is that none of this has noticeably filtered through in any meaningful way into political and economic decision-making around the world, let alone education systems, lifestyles, and ideologies of the people. The dominant root metaphors of Euro-American culture seem as firmly engraved as ever and none of the current developmental pathways open to so-called developing countries breaks in any shape or form from these root metaphors.

I will endeavor in the following pages to document this by analyzing newspaper clippings, research papers, new textbooks in environmental education and education for sustainable development, and UNESCO publications as evidence of my claim. In a second stage I will suggest recommendations on what we can feasibly do to change this situation (which, of course, will be much harder).

Evidence for the Prevalence of Outdated Root Metaphors in European Public Opinion, Research, Environmental Education; Namely, that 'Growth is Necessary'

There is a long history of evidence that continual "growth isn't possible." The latter is the title of a recent publication that makes this evidence accessible in a very convincing manner (Simms and Johnson, 2010). Yet, the entire debate about the financial and ensuing economic crisis was and is always framed within mental models that imply that growth is good and not negotiable. Nearly any daily newspaper proves the point. *The Guardian*, usually highly praised for its environmental reporting, writes:

> Britain's *escape from* recession was *stronger* than previously thought in the final three months of last year, as the services sector *bounced back*. The economy *grew* by 0.3% in the fourth quarter, rather than 0.1% as previously estimated, the Office for National Statistics said this morning. This marked the first time the economy had grown since the first quarter of 2008, when the UK's deepest and longest postwar recession on record began. But city economists, who had penciled in 0.2% growth, said the figures did not change the overall economic picture, which remains weak. Some warned that the economy could slip back into recession in the first three months of

this year. "Certainly a *pleasant surprise for everybody*," wrote Marc Ostwald at Monument Securities. (February 26, 2010)

A careful linguistic analysis of the text reveals that, indeed, anything to do with growth is *positively expressed*, while anything to do with stagnation or even recession is formulated in <u>negative terms</u>. And the highly respected *Neue Zürcher Zeitung*, in fact an agenda-setting media for (neoliberal) economic news, follows suit. As above, I have put the relevant terms in *italics* (positive) and <u>underlined</u> (negative):

> The economic *recovery* in Switzerland <u>loses its dynamic</u>.... The credit and building industries exert a slight <u>negative dynamic</u>. The *recovery* of the Swiss Economy *persists*, but it <u>loses momentum</u>. The index of the Swiss Economic Institute of the Swiss Federal Institute of Technology *increased* in February <u>only</u> by 0.06 points. According to the Institute this means that Swiss Gross National Product will probably *increase* in comparison to the year before, <u>but increasingly less so</u>. The Index had reached an <u>absolute low</u> in April 2009 and after that *increased strongly*. Since October *this positive trend* is <u>weakening</u>.... The signals from Swiss industry and for exports into the U.S. are *positive*; consumption within Switzerland <u>is dwindling though</u>. (February 26, 2010)

This is a clear example where scientific evidence (the first and second law of thermodynamics) proves that the Earth system is materially non-growing and finite. Yet, mainstream economic thinking and, derived from it, public opinion on economic matters, seem unable to "connect the dots." That is, neither the economists nor the public draw the necessary conclusions from a physical reality that has finite resources. As stated above, we are facing the gap between required ecological intelligence and reductionist economic thinking that still claims, in essence, that the economy is autonomous and thus can be conceptualized independently of surrounding systems and their relationships with them.

I firmly believe that the root metaphor of "growth" is the single most important stumbling block to a sustainable future. As this root metaphor provides the conceptual framework supported by other key metaphors, such as individualism, progress, consumerism, and wealth, it needs to be replaced by a more ecologically oriented vocabulary, such as modesty, a sense of limits, humility, and satisfaction with what is actually available on a sustainable basis. This new vocabulary leads to values that will support a modest life that is focused on a less-materialistic lifestyle and is more rewarding in the long run, as promoted by virtually all religions and moral philosophies since ancient times. (Jucker, 2002, pp. 36–37 and 57–59). Since the beginning of the Industrial Revolution, when human-kind started to tap into "stored sunlight" (i.e., fossil fuels, Hartmann, 2001, p. 15), the West's agenda of colonization has put the world on a growth pathway by over-exploiting what clearly doesn't belong just to a few generations. Faster, bigger, higher became the name of the game.

Since the end of the Second World War we have seen exponential growth in virtually all areas. If we look at contemporary life in the West, and now, "thanks" to globalization in much of the world, we will see that the root metaphor of growth permeates the thinking of individuals and governments. A computer is only good enough if it has ever-increasing processing power, data storage capacity, and monitor size. Human qualities are now defined by the number of friends one has on Facebook, or any other so-called social network, even though the number of real friendships upon which one can rely averages below ten. The cars are getting bigger, as are the houses and the number of electronic gadgets in any home. The storage space in MP3-players can now hold more music than one will ever be able to listen to in a lifetime. Everywhere, the emphasis is on growth. We are truly addicted to growth and have totally lost our ability to count the costs of this growth hysteria, let alone its inverse relationship to well-being and quality of life.

A sustainable quality of life is only possible if we shift our entire world-view from a linear and reductionistic one, to a systemic and holistic one. In effect, we need to completely reconfigure our way of thinking about education as well. As I have pointed out elsewhere (Jucker, forthcoming), this re-framing will have to focus on reconceptualizing the assumptions and language underlying the myth of growth by taking account of the context of planetary boundaries. In other words, any education which does not lead to a profound understanding that "the Earth ecosystem is finite, non-growing, materially closed, and while open to the flow of solar energy, that flow is also non-growing and finite" (Daly, 1996, p. 49) and does not make sure that this understanding informs all of what we think and do, cannot in earnest be called an education which contributes to a sustainable future. This means that education which is not systemic on all levels, which does not take us out of the blinding "cocoon" of autonomous thinking and acting units, and does not reflect the fact that our experience of everyday reality consists of layered, interactive, interdependent, self-renewing (sub-) systems, will fail to achieve the necessary reconfiguration. There is a whole set of knowledge areas, skills, values, action competencies, and methods (see Jucker, forthcoming) which need serious attention if we are truly honest about the central aim of the UN Decade on Education for Sustainable Development (hereafter referred to as ESD):

> Reorient the curricula: From pre-school to university, education must be rethought and reformed to be a vehicle of the knowledge, thought patterns and values needed to build a sustainable world. (UNESCO, 2009, p. 7)

The UNESCO guidelines for implementing ESD in teacher training have stated this objective in even starker terms:

> We are faced with a paradox: Is education the problem or the solution in working toward a sustainable future? At current levels of unsustainable practice and over-consumption it could be concluded that education is part of the problem. If education is the solution, then it requires a deeper critique and a broader vision for the future. Thus, whole systems redesign needs to be considered to challenge existing frameworks and shift our thinking beyond current practice and toward a sustainable future. (UNESCO 2005, p. 59)

Until now, what has been missing in the educational efforts to address sustainability is the willingness to question the dominant conceptual model of a growth economy, including the root metaphors that underlie it. Nor has there been a willingness to think systemically about educational reform. I don't see the willingness to "connect the dots." We cannot talk about sustainability while at the same time being silent about planetary boundaries, the double bind of exploiting nature in order to create more affluence, the games being played to safeguard existing illegitimate power structures in politics and the economy, and the propaganda efforts of the media and PR industry to maintain these silences. The post-modern cult of self-interest has obliterated an understanding of the difference between right and wrong, just and unjust, sustainable and unsustainable (all of which are essential in a system defined by limits), and its obsession with "win-win" and "positive approaches" has made it almost impossible to even talk about the above contradictions. These silences signify neither a win nor positive outcomes for the leaders and the affluent middle classes of the world who now stand to lose what they gained through exploitation, arrogance, and neo-colonial attitudes.

These claims can be verified by carefully looking at representative research texts and textbooks. In Kyburz-Graber's textbook on ESD, the entire debate on growth is absent, i.e., silenced. The economic sphere is treated exclusively by equating individual identity with work, and corporate social responsibility and sustainability with innovation (Kyburz-Graber, 2006, p. 81). This means, on the one hand, re-enforcing the root metaphors of the autonomous individual and progress, and, on the other, the inability to arrive at a whole-system perspective that lies outside the narrow boundaries of dialogue allowed by the business community. The textbook also includes the three-circle model of sustainable development which has been introduced in Rio in 1992 by the World Business Council for Sustainable Development and which is wholly inadequate in so far that it posits economy and ecology as equal systems, where, in fact, the former is a sub-system of the latter.

Ironically, an even worse example of ecologically unsustainable thinking can be found in Christine Künzli David's widely read theoretical text on education for sustainable development (2007). The planetary reality of bio-chemical limits is omitted from how the author explains the meaning of sustainable development. As argued above, it is simply anthropocentric hubris to believe that anything other than a functioning biosphere can be the base on which all else depends. No economy or social systems on earth would survive more than a couple of days if Planet Earth were to withdraw all the ecosystem services it provides. Therefore, consistency with natural processes is the name of the game if ever we should achieve a sustainable economy. And, contrary to the belief that human rights are the basis for ESD, only the insight that we live on a single planet with limits raises the questions for justice and equity in a way that goes beyond liberal lip service (*Zukunftsfähiges Deutschland*, 2008, p. 89).

If there are no material limits, the question of justice can be evaded by the promise that one day all will swim in a sea of plenty. But, if that is a physical impossibility, and if we take seriously the declaration of human rights with its proclamation that "all human beings are born free and equal in dignity and rights" (United Nations 1998), then justice and equity are firmly on the agenda. If these ideas are taken seriously, it is then impossible to argue why one person should have a right to more resource use than any other. Whether we like it or not, ecological insights and systems thinking are the very foundation of any meaningful ESD.

Yet in Künzli David's book there is no mention of planetary boundaries. The text even goes further to state that ESD cannot be based on compulsory topics (Künzli David, 2007, p. 76). The recommendation that students construct their own knowledge raises the question of whether it is possible to promote meaningful ESD without focussing on planetary limits and the conflict between the central root metaphors of growth, progress, development, freedom, the autonomous individual, and the need to live within environmental limits. Again, we are presented with post-modern thinking which pretends that there are no such things as physical laws of the planet or criteria by which we can decide whether something is sustainable or not (Künzli David, 2007, p. 35).

Public and educational discourse are now swamped by this attitude that everything is possible and equally valid, and that every opinion counts, even when it is clearly utter nonsense without a shred of evidence supporting it. It is basically a position which refuses to take sides, and shies away from taking a stance on things and stating what is right or wrong (which in most instances is possible, even if there are always exceptions to the rule: organic is better than conventional, wind and solar than nuclear, public transport than the private car, etc.). There is no way Gandhi would have been able to arrive at what in effect was a conception of a sustainable society for India if he had not been very clear about rights and wrongs, dos and don'ts. That we are so thoroughly confused, particularly on moral values, is by no means a surprise, nor has it come about by chance. More than half a century of "democratic anesthesia" (The Invisible Committee, 2007) and concerted political and business propaganda have achieved their aim. People conditioned to be unable to tell right from wrong, and who rely entirely on emotional gut reactions in their political and consumer decisions, are clearly never able to challenge, in any seriousness, the current, illegitimate power structures in our societies and economies (see Chomsky, 1989, 1992, 1994). In order words: We must re-learn to "choose sides" (The Invisible Committee, 2007).

Progress

I have criticized elsewhere the underlying myth of progress which informs a central ESD resource produced by UNESCO, namely, the online ESD tool, "Teaching and Learning for a Sustainable Future" (see Jucker, 2003). My analysis uncovered a startlingly uncritical attitude toward how western science/technology has been based on the myth of progress, as well as an even more far-reaching naïve advocacy of ICT (Information and Communication Technology) and the internet as learning tools for ESD.

What has gone largely unnoticed is the problematic nature of the linear pattern of thinking reinforced by the root metaphor of progress which sacrifices all tradition and all indigenous oral knowledge and understanding on the altar of "the new." Change, it seems, is always better, even though on balance it is clear to see that change (as introduced by the Industrial Revolution) has brought upon us destruction on a planetary scale that was previously unimaginable, and which is clearly threatening to cancel out any true gains and positive developments which have undoubtedly been made as well. As evidence of the imbalance between genuine contributions and environmental destruction, it is necessary to consider how all forms of life are now being impacted by the synthetic chemicals that were introduced in the name of progress.

It is interesting to note that neither research texts nor textbooks on ESD directly engage with this central aspect of sustainability, namely, that our Euro-American model of progress is fundamentally unsustainable. By not overtly putting this topic on the table, they are effectively silencing the debate (see Künzli David, 2007, Kyburz-Graber, et al., 2006). Künzli David goes even a step further in promoting the myth of progress. Ironically, just before the paragraph in which she states that ESD "is not allowed to propose a fixed concept" of sustainable development, she mandates that sustainable development must be conceptualized "in a positive and optimistic manner" (2007, p. 34). There is simply no way that we can legislate this. What a transition to a sustainable society requires is a systemic and honest analysis of the unsustainability of the current situation and of solutions that are systemically coherent and consistent with the non-negotiable planetary boundaries. The results can be positive or negative, depending on whether you win (most likely poor people) or lose (most likely Euro-American consumers), and this will undoubtedly influence your optimistic or pessimistic outlook. What needs to be emphasized is that her research textbook claims to lay sound foundations for ESD in Switzerland and German-speaking countries in general. Yet, if we look at the ecological footprint of Switzerland and agree with David Selby that we shouldn't so much talk about education for sustainable development but, rather, about education for sustainable contraction (Selby 2007), we know that we in Euro-American societies will face a lot of "despair, pain, grief and loss" (Selby, 2007, p. 259). How will we be able to cope with this reality if we adhere to the dogma of being only "positive and optimistic"?

Autonomous Individualism and Freedom

> Someone who is poking around in the fog of his or her own self is no longer capable of noticing that this isolation, this 'solitary confinement of the ego' is a mass sentence—that millions of people in all the highly industrialized countries are also pacing the prison cells of the self. (Ulrich Beck, quoted in Adbusters, Vol. 18, No. 2, issue 88, March/April 2010)

> In France, the ferocious and secular work of individualization by the power of the state, that classifies, compares, disciplines and separates its subjects starting from a very young age, that instinctively grinds down any solidarities that escape it until nothing remains except citizenship—a pure, phantasmic sense of belonging to the Republic. (The Invisible Committee, 2007)

As argued earlier, it is obvious that our Euro-American conception of the autonomous individual serves very important ideological, political, and economic functions. But the excessive reliance upon materialistic values has turned the emphasis on individualism into the driving force behind exploitative capitalism and bourgeois democracy. Yet, it is not a conception which can stand up to the realities of life on our planet. Unfortunately, it is, apart from the root metaphors of growth and progress, probably the most ingrained of all, and it translates seamlessly into this other fallacious western liberal notion of individual freedom which is in serious need of being reconceptualized in ways that take account of analogs informed by environmental limits and an understanding of how other cultures have learned to exercise ecological intelligence. We need to ask the question: How much freedom—or, to be more precise, which kind of freedom is still possible on the blue planet with its population fast approaching seven billion? (Martin/Schumann, 1997, p. 28). Especially in Euro-American consumer societies, freedom is interpreted as a *carte blanche* to do whatever your fancy might desire. As

Bowers observed, "only a culture that regards the individual as auto-nomous can propagate a view of individual reality within a context free from social accountability, much less accountability to the 'off-line' biotic community that sustains individual life" (Bowers, 2000, p. 32). "Given the physical and social limits we all experience, the very idea of absolute freedom is, strictly speaking, absurd. Without recognizable limits, a defi-nition of freedom is empty and meaningless." (Marshall, 1993, p. 39)

Within the context of sustainability, and on the basis of the earth's life-support systems, it is clearly the case that we need a notion of free-dom which understands both the bio-chemical limits of the biosphere *and* the respective freedom of the other inhabitants and future genera-tions. Sachs has put it succinctly: "Only self-limitation can lead to real self-liberation" (Sachs, 1999, p. 186). The liberal notion of absolute, free-floating freedom of the autonomous individual, whereby everybody can fulfill their every whim, is essentially a negative freedom. That is, it is freedom from responsibilities toward anybody and anything. Freedom cannot be properly understood in an anthropocentric and individually centered way, and is self-defeating as an end in itself. It is not the well-being and self-determined interests of the individual that are of central concern; rather, the freedom of the individual stands in the service of, and is limited by, the integrity of the biosphere and the continuation of the human community supported by it.

Yet, if we look into contemporary research and textbooks on ESD, we find that its entire conceptual basis is informed by the dominant hegemony of constructivism, which is based on this fallacious notion of the autonomous individual. This can be seen most clearly in the discus-sion of key competencies where the agenda has been articulated by the OECD (essentially a lobbying organization for the interests of global capitalism). The three categories of key competencies identified by this organization seem, at first glance, to be highly useful. After all, one cate-gory is called "Interacting in Heterogeneous Groups," and the one called "Acting Autonomously" is immediately qualified: "Acting autonomously does not mean functioning in social isolation." (OECD, 2005, p. 14) If the document is read carefully, which includes being aware of the underlying conceptual models, it quickly becomes apparent that the world is seen exclusively through the eyes of individuals, and understood on the basis of their limited experiences. There is no awareness of the interrelationships stressed by Bateson, let alone the notion that:

> The total self-corrective unit which processes information, or, as I say, 'thinks' and 'acts' and 'decides,' is a *system* whose boundaries do not at all coincide with the boundaries either of the body or of what is popularly called the 'self' or 'consciousness'; and it is important to notice that there are *multiple* differences between the thinking system and the 'self' as popularly conceived. (Bateson, 2000, p. 319)

The underlying understanding in the OECD document is that there is such a thing as an autonomous, independent, self-determined unit called an "individual," almost like a monad in Leibniz's sense. It is also important to note that the opposition to the self-determined individual is represented as the "crowd"—a pejorative metaphor.

> Individuals *must* act autonomously in order to participate effectively in the development of society and to function well in different spheres of life…. This is because they need to develop *independently* an *identity* and to make choices, rather than just follow the crowd. (OECD, 2005, p. 14; italics added)

In the introduction to the document, there is also a list of criteria all key competencies must meet. Here, again, it becomes clear that even society is only conceptualized as a collection of individuals (and not the other way round). The list reads as follows. Each key competency must:

- Contribute to valued outcomes for societies and individuals;
- Help individuals meet important demands in a wide variety of contexts; and
- Be important not just for specialists, but for all individuals. (OECD, 2005, p. 4)

The entire debate about individualizing teaching/learning and streaming different levels of ability, which is still at the heart of questions about educational reforms in Europe, is based on this notion that education has no other purpose than to yield the perfect, fully functional, and self-directing autonomous person.

The ESD text widely used in Switzerland clearly argues for a constructivist approach to learning. The key understanding is based on the assumption that learners are actively in control of their learning. To quote from the textbook, "Learning is an active, self-directed, constructivist, situated and socially embedded process" (Künzli David, 2007, p. 38). Learners, according to constructivist theory, avoid being influenced by how the language of the culture into which they are born carries forward the assumptions and patterns of thinking of earlier eras. Instead, youthful learners rely upon their own autonomous thought processes in making sense of their experiences, in deciding what questions to ask, and in deciding what values should guide their behavior toward other autonomous individuals. As summarized in the ESD text, "The construction of knowledge is a purely individual activity" (Künzli David, 2007, p. 39). This ideologically driven view of learning then leads to arguing that "ESD contributes to individuals who can orientate themselves as independent persons in the world" (Künzli David, 2007, 58). Thus, educational reform is to start with how "the pupils feel responsible, know and are able to act" (Künzli David, 2007, pp. 59–64). No other cultural or natural system influences are to be considered. The discussion of the aims of ESD ends with the assertion that "In order to contribute to sustainable development it is necessary to reach individual knowledge through personal reflection." (Künzli David, 2007, p. 67)

The following point needs to be made. The above critical discussion is not meant as a personal attack on the authors. In a sense, the researchers and writers cannot be held entirely responsible as they were socialized by previous generations of teachers and professors who ignored that their abstract ideas about freedom, growth, and a human-centered world were already contributing to the degradation of the earth's natural systems. It seems clear that the advocates of ESD reforms are reproducing —as claimed in the above chapters—the metaphorical thinking taken for granted by their professors. The irony is that they failed to recognize the contradiction between their own educational experience and their argument that the goal of education is to promote a process of thinking that is free of cultural influences. What Bateson refers to as the recursive nature of thinking, as well as how the metaphorical nature of language carries forward the patterns of thinking that were intended to address the problems of previous eras, raises the question of whether the promoters of ESD have a responsibility to question the earlier misconceptions encoded in the vocabulary that is central to their reform proposals. It would seem obvious that the metaphors of growth, freedom, and individualism can no longer be reconciled with understanding the current condition of the interdependent cultural and natural ecologies. What these ESD reformers need is a firm grounding in whole-systems thinking and ecological intelligence, but this means not being guided by an ideology that is based on the abstractions that led to the development of the Industrial Revolution. As a consequence of not being grounded in systems-thinking and an understanding of ecological intelligence, they think in their "educational studies" box and apply it to ESD without realizing that the analogs that frame the meaning of their guiding metaphors don't work anymore and are even contradictory.

Conclusion

It is a truly astonishing thing. In education, we submit wholesale to the idea of the autonomous individual and to the corresponding ideology of constructivism. While elsewhere in life, it is clear that we get nowhere with this idea. It is by now well proven that to learn any craft or trade or musical instrument to a competent level requires at least 10,000 hours, or roughly ten years, of practice (Sennett, 2008). Closely connected with this insight is the understanding that we don't start off as autonomous, self-directed, independent people, but that we are deeply *dependent* on significant others, such as an elder or a mentor who is at the master's level already and has the necessary life experiences. All indigenous societies and most eastern philosophers know that only through a period of being mentored by an experienced and wise master of the craft will we stand a chance of becoming human beings capable of mastering a profession and having a quality of life, not just on a technical level, but also as morally responsible people. Take love. Here the same is true. We cannot ever fulfill our deepest desires alone and we cannot learn to love in a day or by taking a self-training course. So why do we propose such absurd ideas in education?

I am not quite sure what to suggest as solutions to the problems outlined above. I feel a distinct sense of helplessness when I think about all these root metaphors which urgently need to be reconfigured within the perspective of an ecological intelligence. I have written almost excessively about it (see, for example, Jucker, 2002 and 2008), yet all I ever had to say repeated the wisdom of others. People like Mahatma Gandhi, Wendell Berry, Vandana Shiva, E.F. Schumacher, Wolfgang Sachs, Herman Daly, and many others, have said pretty much the same things far more convincingly (another proof that we are nothing except what we become through interrelations with others). Yet, we are clearly not getting the message across; nor do we seem to be making any inroads. If the hegemonic root metaphors and discourse in politics, economics, and education are deeply unsustainable and incompatible with ecological intelligence, then I am more and more convinced that Chris Hedges' analysis is correct:

> All resistance must recognize that the body politic and global capitalism are dead. We should stop wasting energy trying to reform or appeal to them. This does not mean the end of resistance, but it does mean very different forms of resistance. It means turning our energies toward building sustainable communities to weather the coming crisis, since we will be unable to survive and resist without a cooperative effort. (Hedges, 2010, p. 15)

Particularly in the context of education for a sustainable future, this means that we need to practice the systemic insights which we can glean from Bateson. Either we build coherent sustainable communities based on practices informed by ecological intelligence, or we will suffer the consequences of the systemic failures of the current system.

CHAPTER 9

Revitalizing the Ecological Intelligence of Andean Amazonian Communities: The Way Back to Respect

By Jorge Ishizawa and Grimaldo Rengifo, Co-directors,
Proyecto Andino de Tecnologías Campesinas (PRATEC), Lima, Peru

Ecological and Historical Background

In his deeply sensitive reading of Hölderlin's poem that contains the lines "… poetically, man dwells on this earth…," German philosopher Martin Heidegger (1971) shows that ecological intelligence is not alien to western traditions. Why and when did this tradition lose its currency is a question we intend to take up here only insofar as it pertains to our lands, the central Andes comprising Ecuador, Perú, and Bolivia.

In Felipe Fernández-Armesto's *Civilizations*, we find the following quote from *Historia del Nuevo Mundo I* (1653), where Father Bernabé Cobo, a seventeenth-century Spanish chronicler and a remarkable naturalist, puts in writing, perhaps for the first time in history, the "colonizing gaze" of the Andean highlands:

> As a result of the excessive cold which produces killing frosts, none of the lands of the high sierra can be used to grow fruits and vegetables… and we can even include here a good measure of the land at the next level of altitude, which also has uninhabitable stretches… Because of the composition of the soil, there are lands which, although they have a good climate, are yet unsuitable for cultivation… because some of these mountains have numerous crags and rough, brambly ground covering many leagues. Other mountains have good soil, but they are so rugged and lofty that they cannot be worked. All of these causes make most of these Indies impossible to cultivate or live in, as I have noted often when travelling through many of these provinces. (2000, p. 271)

From this viewpoint, the extraordinary ecological diversity present in these lands (80% of life zones existing on the planet) is seen as an obstacle, not only to progress and well-being, but even inimical to life itself. Hence, it was the abundant presence of minerals in the Andean mountain range that attracted the attention of the Spanish invaders and made the country known in Europe through the expression "It's worth a Peru!" to refer to a wonderful bounty of gold and silver. Thus, during the time of Spanish colonization, the central Andes was mining country. A flourishing civilization was thwarted in its development and replaced by a colonial rule that decimated the native population in the territories of the Americas. It is reported that one out of ten survived in the central Andes, while one out of twenty-five survived in Mexico and Brazil. This "colonizing gaze" has persisted during the past five centuries and has become the official view held by governments since independence from Spanish rule in the early nineteenth century down to our days.

How Are We to Understand 'Ecological Intelligence' in the Central Andes?

The Chilean biologists Humberto Maturana and Gloria Guiloff propose an approach to intelligence that starts:

> From accepting [two assumptions]:
> 1. That there is a class of behavior exhibited by animals in general, and by man in particular, that involves the interactions of two or more organisms or the interactions of an organism and its medium, that an observer calls intelligent behavior; and
> 2. That the word 'intelligence' is used by the observer to make a connotative reference to the relations and changes of relations that take place between the systems participating in this behavior, without denoting a particular property or attribute of the individual organisms, or without denoting a particular feature of the individual performances... [Thus,] intelligent behavior is viewed as a conduct whose peculiarity consists in that it is enacted in a particular context as a result of a particular history of interactions of the acting organism with other organisms or with its medium. (1980, p. 137)

In our case, what we can make of their proposal is that ecological intelligence is displayed by human communities inhabiting particular ecosystems in a way that furthers their continuing structural coupling with "other organisms [and] with its medium."

Development and Colonization

Ecological intelligence is not a salient feature of colonization. As a part of Latin America, the central Andes have been a generous and continuous provider of means for the development of capitalism since its inception. They still are. Although there was no change in the results, development projects led and globalized by the United States in the second half of the twentieth century, enthused and galvanized the minds of university graduates all over the globe, including ours.

What remained invisible to the "colonizing gaze" was the continuing existence of indigenous communities that managed to support themselves and the masses of successive invaders by relying on their own tradition of nurturing the plants, animals, and wild spaces in the exacting circumstances of life in the high mountains. The reason is probably that this gaze focused on the fertile plains as appropriate to agriculture. Fertile plains are scarce in the Peruvian Andes and are restricted to the narrow coastal valleys formed and irrigated by the 52 rivers, of which only one is permanent throughout the year, that produce oases in the desertic coast starting in the high mountains and fertilizing the Pacific Ocean. In the Peruvian highlands there are only three medium-size valleys: the Sacred valley of Cusco in the southern Sierra, the Mantaro valley in the central Sierra, and the Cajamarca valley in the northern Sierra. To the colonizing gaze it was invisible that the indigenous agriculture, with all its diversity and variability of species, varieties and ecosystems, and the sophisticated tuning of diverse communities to this reality, took place in the steep slopes of the Andean mountain range.

The colonizing gaze installed itself at the universities in the central Andes where knowledge of agriculture and related rural development studies were imparted under what Ward Churchill called a White Studies regime. In Perú, this was disseminated from Europe, specifically from the prestigious agricultural school at Gembloux, Belgium, wherefrom the founders of the first agricultural school in Perú came on a mission at the beginning of the twentieth century. Since the 1950s, droves of agronomists joined the Green Revolution to carry out the modernization of Peruvian agriculture, based on the knowledge proper to cultivating the plains, and neglecting the specific characteristics of the Andean highlands. Before the military government's agrarian reform in 1969, the coastal and highland *haciendas* hired professionals to exploit the fertile plains where modern agriculture could thrive. Thus, export crops like sugar cane and cotton came to be cultivated in the coastal *haciendas*, and modern husbandry for wool, milk, and meat was installed in the highland *haciendas*. Crops for sustenance were left to be cultivated on the Andean slopes considered as marginal lands.

During the period of agrarian reform, with the recovery of the lands in the highlands by the indigenous communities and the demise of the *hacienda* system, the demands for technical personnel in the rural development professions changed. Development projects required technical personnel knowledgeable in local agricultural practices, but the agrarian universities were not prepared for this change. In spite of the fact that the enrollment of the Faculty of Agronomy included mainly young people from highland communities (90% in Ayacucho and 85% in Cajamarca), the curriculum did not include courses on peasant Andean agriculture. In an interview, the late Sergio Cuzco, an agronomist from Cajamarca in the northern highlands, gave testimony to the challenge that confronted any attempt that purported the recovery of the communities' indigenous ecological intelligence:

> When we left the university, we tried to introduce all the innovations we had learned in the work we carried out with the NGO. We had resources; we could afford the *minga* [contribution to the common fund in collective work]; we provided some food. The peasants accepted all of it saying 'It's OK.' Soon we realized that all the common work achieved was ruined by the *campesinos* themselves. We were distracted a little and what we had done was no longer there... Having left the NGO in frustration, we visited the *campesinos* and then they said very frankly that we were wrong. I learned that they had to decide how they were going to improve the *chacra* [cultivated field]. So what followed was an extended effort to learn from the *campesinos*. To engage in a relationship of equivalence with the *campesinos*... we got a *chacra* and we established a different relationship with them, based on reciprocity [and involvement]: We help them; they help us. What we get from outside the community is for the *ayni* [collective labor]... We are strengthening what the *campesinos* do. We tell them: What you choose to improve should be according to your understanding of how the *chacra* must be done. It is a strengthening of their thinking, of their practices. We do not propose blueprints, because we are very much aware that the *chacras* are not the same, because the *campesinos* conduct them according to their own understanding and possibilities. (PRATEC, 1993a, pp. 140–141)

It was clear that it was not a matter of methodology and contents in the agronomists' knowledge. It was its impertinence, its total abstraction of the place, an acute case of "misplaced concreteness" in Whitehead's telling expression. Or, as Bateson would put it, the cultural maps of the colonizers reduced the "territory" (the local cultural and natural systems) to what could be economically exploited. The native source of the knowledge appropriate for good living in the place and circumstances had been rendered invisible.

At the time (the 1990s), PRATEC was developing a training program whose vision was to find people who could accompany the *campesino* communities as Sergio had. For this reason, it was clear that participants with extensive field experience were to provide the anchor for all of the course's endeavors. But that experience had to address the question each participant brought to the course: How do I start accompanying communities? Néstor Chambi, an Aymara agronomist who pioneered cultural affirmation in the altiplano area ("re-ethnification," he called it), started, in the later years of the 1980s, conversing with his parents and with community elders about their customs and knowledge. Néstor remembers his visits to don Pedro Toque from the community of Japisse in the district of Conima, his hometown:

> We talked the whole day. I took coca leaves and some bread with me and we spent the whole day conversing... He said: *How have I longed to tell these things and no one would listen. My children do not care, my grandchildren even less... I thought I will die with all I know....* He asked: *Who has sent you? Surely someone has sent you.* I always remember that he said that I was being like a balm, a medicine, helping him get rid of a load that prevented him from speaking. I felt likewise. He willingly talked of the *ayllus*, of our organization, of our customs, of how our celebrations used to be, about the authorities' and people's clothing, everything. He even told stories... We talked for three days, and I thought that I could be bothering him so I proposed to come back later. He replied: *Now I can die in peace.* I was deeply moved and his words have always given me strength and determination. (Chuyma Aru, 2006)

The Agro-Festive Calendar and Community Lifeworld: The Cultural Transmission of Ecological Intelligence

Going to the elders was a crucial step in the recovery of the community ecological intelligence lost during the years of university studies.

What is the world that we are inheriting? What we found is its central agro-centric character. In spite of Father Cobo's assessment, successive generations populated the Andes, nurturing plants and animals that constituted, over a time span of at least eight millennia, a world center of agriculture, presently reputed as the one with the richest agro-biodiversity on the planet.

PRATEC started its activities with the aim of collecting ancestral agricultural knowledge in the form of practices of nurturance and has carried on this activity for more than two decades. The practices are documented in technological booklets, and, more recently, using diverse audiovisual formats. The first collections helped to show that, contrary to university teaching claiming its obsolescence, the practices were a very vital part of *campesino* life. The first practices documented were mainly ancestral techniques for preparing the soil, sowing, crop association, and infrastructure like terraces, etc. Gradually, it was recognized that the practices could not be properly appreciated without taking account of the importance of community festivals, rituals, and celebrations, where music and dance were vital expressions of the human community's conversation with its deities for the propitiation of climatic harmony, and hence, for harvest security.

In these two past decades it has turned out that one useful way of organizing an interpretation of the ecological intelligence of the communities is through the graphic representation of their agro-festive calendar, where activities mark the different events in the agricultural cycle. Initially utilized for the incorporation of local knowledge in the school curriculum, the agro-festive calendar has been widely adopted throughout the educational system in the central Andean countries.

A complementary representation is that of the local landscape with its diverse ecological zones. This representation orders the observations at the levels of the ecosystems, agriculture (*chacra* and *kanchas*), inter- and intra-specific diversity, and their interrelations (PAR, 2010, p. 20). With this framework, the testimonies from *campesinos* in different places in the Peruvian Andes and Upper Amazon regions help flesh out an interpretation of their understanding of their life world, providing leads to their cosmovision.

Signs

"Climatic indicators" is the technical denomination of what the *campesinos* translate as *señas* (signs) in Spanish. Conversation among all those who inhabit a *pacha*, or local world, is mainly through signs for the purpose of mutual tuning and understanding to decide what, where, and how to sow to secure the harvests for the sustenance of humans, animals, and deities, and even for the deceased. Some signs are plants, animals, birds, fish, reptiles and amphibians, meteors and other phenomena, festivals and rituals. Doña Lucía Coaquira Callo, from the community of Lakasani in the northern part of the altiplano by Lake Titikaka, says: "The *leqe leqes* [birds] have arrived and the *ch'eje* [Pleiades] is rising in the sky. Surely, frost will begin to fall very hard; we should now make *chuño* [potato dehydrated through exposure to sun and frost]." (Cutipa, 2006, p. 1) "To obtain *chuño* several types of beings participate: humans, signs (animals, plants, heavenly bodies, etc.), snowfall, rain, wind, frost, sun, deities, beginning with soil preparation for sowing potato, up to ritually and festively storing *chuño*," Cutipa comments.

In the Quechua area of Quispillaccta, doña Julia Núñez Huamaní asserts:

> There are signs for everything to advise you. For rain, I look at the *chiwillu* Santa Rosa because when it is in *qachwa* [shrieking and getting excited] in circles it is to continue raining, but when the black *chiwillu* is in *qachwa* and in circles, it is for rain to stop. We look at and listen to everything. In these days [early September] the fox is howling clearly. There is going to be a good harvest of *oca*, not as last year when its howl was raucous and interrupted. (ABA, 2001, p. 99)

Agricultural Practices

In the 1980s, agricultural practices constituted the core of what used to be known as Andean traditional technology. Its collection and documentation made clear the specific character of Andean *campesino* agriculture. Rather than calling it "agriculture," as it is known in other places and latitudes, the *campesino* communities refer to it as "mutual nurturance." Julia Pacoricona Aliaga from Conima, Puno, clarifies it in reference to her relationship with the potato plant:

> The potato is our mother because when it produces fruits, it is feeding us, clothing us, and giving us happiness, but we also nurture it. When they are small, we call them *wawas* [children] because we have to look after them, delouse [weed] them, clothe [hill soil to] them,

make them dance and feast with them. This has always been done. My parents taught me to nurture them with affection and good will as we do with our children. (terre des hommes, 2001, p. 23)

PRATEC's collection of agricultural practices now numbers more than three thousand technological booklets; in reading them it becomes clear how nurturance permeates all activities in the chacra (cultivated field) like sowing crops in mixed varieties, and in the landscape. In the latter case, its nurturance is oriented to the creation of hospitable niches for plants and animals by terracing and building stone walls to enclose pastures.

Ecological Governance and Community Ecological Intelligence
In the Andean highlands, topography has conditioned the occupation of territory by families possessing plots in several ecological zones. Thus, population has been generally dispersed throughout the landscape. Enacting community in these lands has always been crucial for "living in sufficiency," as the Quispillacctas characterize their well-being. Community is expressed in the traditional conception of authority:

> Exercising authority is to be part of a family with all the members of the community. It is to be *taytamama* [father and mother] of all. *Uma* [head] is the couple that leads the nurturance of all, that facilitates the conversation with climate, water, heavenly bodies, with whom we share the nurturing of all. They are in charge of dissolving conflicts, of bringing harmony. Authority is exercised in an environment of closeness and affection. You perceive in the members of the community a very close relationship. They call the authorities *papay* or *mamay* even if they are not of the same blood because we are all related by affection; all are family; all share the responsibility of being *taytamama* during the exercise of their charges. (ABA, 2001, p. 198)

It is not only humans who exercise authority. At the regional level:

> Seeds, as authority, compensate for the abundance or lack of *Kawsay* [seed, food] of several communities, but at the same time, new families commit themselves to share other activities; they will share their crop in another moment. Thus, they facilitate the renewal of collective life and contribute to the flourishing of relationships between *ayllus* and communities. Seeds, as authority for the wider

region, are who determine the organization of the activities of the families, of the *ayllu*, and the intercommunity relationships in the region. Seeds facilitate the organization of life in the region. Its manifestation is the seed exchange that enriches local and regional diversity. (*ibid.*, p. 185)

Cultural Affirmation Is the Recovery of Ecological Intelligence: the Nuclei for Andean Amazonian Cultural Affirmation (NACA)

Instead of its avowed goal of mainstreaming peasant indigenous agriculture in universities, PRATEC's course provided the impetus for the formation of community-based local NGOs spread throughout the country (16, at the latest count). There was no blueprint for them although the example of pioneering NACAs like Sergio's or Néstor's inspired the accompaniment of all succeeding NACAs. A two-tiered approach gradually developed in which these local community-based organizations, or Nuclei for Andean Amazonian Cultural Affirmation, undertook the accompaniment of the communities in their agro-centric recovery of ecological intelligence, while PRATEC took over the technical coordination and management of joint projects oriented to the strengthening of rural communities which practice traditional agriculture. Coordination consisted of convening periodic meetings for the exchange of experiences among the NACAs and for sharing reflections on a common theme of pressing interest in the projects. These reflections were submitted by the NACAs as essays which were compiled, edited, and published by PRATEC. The other centralized activity was the annual course on Andean *campesino* agriculture. There has been a synergic relationship between the activities in the two tiers. Over the years, PRATEC has exercised an intellectual coordination that initially consisted of the circulation of an essay on the theme of the year, inviting the NACAs to converse on the issues that involved the communities they accompanied. More recently, the coordination has consisted of the identification of community processes that elders consider worth reinforcing and making proposals for joint action.

Something that appeared very early in this setup is the importance of follow-up as a close mutual accompaniment, which goes back to the inception of the annual course, that is, before the formation of the NACAs. The course was only the beginning of a long-term involvement.

The impacts of the PRATEC courses can only be appreciated in this context. The mutual nurturance could be actualized on occasions when shared projects provided the space and topic for joint reflection and further mutual enrichment. Until July 1995, PRATEC accompanied two local NGOs, one in Ayacucho (ABA) and another in Puno (Chuyma Aru), integrated by former course graduates who had returned to their communities of origin and animated the revival of their tradition of Andean agriculture and governance. A program funded by the German Ministry for Cooperation and Development (BMZ), and mediated by the German international NGO, terre des hommes (tdh), allowed PRATEC to facilitate the creation of six new NACAs (in addition to the existing two) in the first phase (1995–1998), with two new NACAs joining in the second phase (1999–2001). The NACAs were formed to support cultural affirmation in the communities. PRATEC encouraged their autonomy, both from the administrative and financial points of view. The annual course not only provided the formation of the NACAs' personnel, but was also a space of reflection and actualization of what was being learned from supporting the Andean Amazonian communities of nurturers of the diversity of plants and animals. There has been constant feedback between the course and the projects. Participants of the early classes have stayed with the course to continue their reflections on what they are learning in the field as they help nurture the new course participants. At the same time, the course provides space for reflection on the local efforts, within the global context, to base development on the wisdom of our Andean Amazonian communities.

A program for the *in situ* conservation of native-cultivated plants and their wild relatives, originating in Perú—the world center of biological diversity—started in January 2001, with PRATEC coordinating a network of 10 NACAs. As a GEF-funded project, with the local administration of the United Nations Development Program (UNDP), the implementation of the In Situ Project, as it was nicknamed, involved five other public and private participants: two state organizations and three NGOs over a period of five years (2001–2005). The program's results attest to the existence of an extraordinary repository of biological diversity in the Peruvian Andes and Amazonia, and to the inextricable link between this diversity and that of the communities of the Andean Amazonian nurturers of biodiversity. The program documented the traditional knowledge of the nurturance of native plants and their wild relatives, including the governance systems that promote the regeneration of agro-biodiversity.

Almost simultaneously, another two-phased educational program (2002–2007) under the heading of Children and Biodiversity (Ch&B) started, once again funded by the BMZ, facilitated by terre des homes—Germany, and involving seven NACAs—two of which also participated in the In Situ Project. The Ch&B program focus became the incorporation of local traditional knowledge into the curriculum of 35 rural schools in the Andes and Amazonia. The initial overall goal was to promote the community's nurturance of the school, reversing the growing discord between the rural school and the community over the past five decades. What has become clear from our conversations with community elders throughout the Andes, since 2000, is that the school has been instrumental in furthering a generalized loss of respect in the communities; towards nature, towards the deities through a neglect of rituals and celebrations, and toward the elders by contesting their traditional authority. When asked if schools in rural areas should help promote the urban kind of knowledge or their own knowledge, the unanimous answer has been: *"Iskay Yachay"* [both kinds of knowledge in the Quechua language] or *"Paya Yatiwi"* [in Aymara]. What seems to be present in the Andean Amazonian communities is the radical demand for cultural diversity (Ishizawa and Rengifo, 2009).

The Yachaq Network: Regeneration of Community Ecological Intelligence

A promising outcome of the Ch&B program has been the initiative of community elders, in the altiplano district of Juli in Puno, to form an informal network called *Suma Uta* ("hospitable abode," in the Aymara language) in order to provide the community counterpart to *Paya Yatiwi*. Nelguardo Huanca, one of its members, explained the reasons:

> Why is *Paya Yatiwi* important? Because the children will learn to 'pass life.' For *Paya Yatiwi* is not only the teachers' task, nor only the parents.' If only one of them is wanted, we'd be lost. For *Paya Yatiwi* to go well, both must work together. But we need to strengthen it because external help is not eternal. We are the ones who will remain in the community; we have to set the example. (Rengifo, 2008)

The *yachaq* network has been active in the teaching of community skills in the schools in Juli. It has also been invited to share its experience in schools in Cusco, and in communities in several places in Bolivia. *Yachaq*-to-*yachaq* exchanges are very effective means whose results we expect to eventually inform regional and national educational policies.

Two additional programs, the Fund for Andean Amazonian Cultural Affirmation Initiatives (FIAC), involving 10 NACAs (2002–2009), and the *Sallqa* project (2005–2007) involving two NACAs in the central highlands region, were major contributors to what we consider to be the experiential base for our reflections in this paper. FIAC was funded by the Geneva Federation for Cooperation and Development (GFCD) and constitutes what we believe to be an alternative to state intervention for rural poverty alleviation. Instead of a development-style external provision of know-what and know-how, FIAC was based on the community's understanding of their needs and ways of meeting them. That restricted external intervention to a limited number of inputs of urban origin through microprojects.

The *Sallqa* (wild spaces) project had the auspices of Swedbio, the Swedish international biodiversity program during the period 2005–2007, and dealt with the question of ecosystem services within the framework of the Millennium Ecosystem Assessment (MEA). The project's objective was to look into the high Andean communities' understanding of the concept of ecosystem services. Rather than focusing on what nature offers humans, they concentrated on what Andean communities do to ensure the continuous provision of such services.

While the In Situ and Ch&B projects were thematically focused on biodiversity conservation and rural education, respectively, the FIAC and *Sallqa* projects allowed us to realize the extent and depth of the Andean Amazonian communities' concerns. As had been the case with the Ch&B program, the generalized loss of respect was the foremost concern. FIAC's motto actually became "Back to respect," a call that has been repeated again and again in our conversations with community elders throughout the Andes. In fact, it has been dominant in the ongoing exploration that we have jointly undertaken with the NACAs on the communities' understanding of the climate crisis. The elders attribute the crisis to a loss of respect towards nature. Once again, it is an invitation to go "Back to respect."

A retrospective look at both programs makes us aware of the depth of the *yachaqs'* knowledge, now variously called traditional, community, or local knowledge at the international conventions on Biological Diversity and the Combat against Desertification. The traditional practices of cultivation and nurturance and the application of ancestral forms of governance led to our identification of the root cause of a developing emergency by the Andean Amazonian communities, and their actions to deal with it. An examination of the microprojects undertaken by communities of the central meridional Peruvian highlands, for instance, indicated that 82% of the total number of microprojects related to aspects of the climatic emergency, from the recovery of ancestral authorities and precious cultivators, to water harvesting and irrigation works (PRATEC, 2010). Communities did not wait for the scientific community to reach agreement as to the existence and extent of the climate crisis before acting in accordance to their own understanding and know how.

UniVida: the University for Life as a Proposal for the Regeneration of Ecological Intelligence in the Central Andes

In our lands it is a common experience to meet very capable people who have no academic background. For various reasons, formal respectability has eluded them in making their life according to their calling. When asked where they acquired their marvelous skills, they would respond that they "did it in the University of Life" (just by living). Be it in the handicrafts, agriculture, industry, cooking, music and dance, sciences or trades, life demanded of them to be *canchis oficio*, to exercise the community's seven skills. We have learned that it is not a quantitative matter; "seven" can mean three or eleven: they are the skills that help you to "pass life," to be able to be in the minds of the community when something is to be done. To "pass life" requires the attitude of someone who is ready to "command by obeying," in the telling Zapatista injunction.

UniVida is the form that our exploration in the ways of intergenerational transmission of ecological intelligence has taken. It was prompted by the demands of the young Quechua community members in the Upper Amazon region of San Martin. They were eager to affirm their traditional culture while opening themselves to learning from a world characterized by cultural diversity. They feel that the present demands the acquisition of a diversity of skills and knowledge based on their own culture.

Once again through Germany's support, the initial effort of a two-year (2009–2010) program implemented by four NACAs, in San Martín, Ayacucho, Cusco, and Puno, allowed us to glimpse the potential of the idea.

Inspired by Mexico's Uniterra, or Earth University, UniVida provides a space where teachers and learners meet. No bureaucracy, classrooms, or supervisors are present, only those who have a taste for sharing what they know and those who want to acquire a skill that the community values are in the workshops, *chacras* (cultivated fields), forests and rivers. Learning happens when one does what one wants to learn with someone who guides the hand, not "putting chains to the spirit, but holding a hand," as Jorge Luis Borges, the Argentinian writer, expresses it.

UniVida was not created to institutionalize the spontaneous forms of learning in life, nor for schooling or deschooling society, but to accompany the existing urban and rural communities' initiatives, strengthening the relationships of those who want to learn and those willing to teach in a personal and equal relationship.

UniVida sees itself as an indigenous project. The characteristics of a good community member are embodied in Gustavo Esteva's account of an eighteenth-century Quechua leader: "Juan Chiles was a wise man because he knew how to unknot the Quechua language, how to read Charlemagne's books, and how to plow using a cord (*labrar a cordel*)." This expression means that:

• One should know the web of life and unknot it, communicating with other peoples through the Quechua language;
• One should know the ideas, laws, and thoughts of other peoples; and
• One should know how to do things well, rightly, and so that they are useful for life.

UniVida is an agro-centric proposal, making the indigenous peasant nurturance of the diversity of plants, animals, and ecosystems the privileged space for life and learning. It reaffirms the vocation of these lands for agriculture and the priority that rural life should have in the understanding of good living on the planet. By focusing on the chacra, UniVida opens to the diversity of options of good living by making *Iskay Yachay / Paya Yatiwi* (two kinds of knowledge) an educational reality.

SCHOOLS FOR LIVING DIVERSITY

In UniVida, school does not mean classrooms. The schools for living diversity are places for the regeneration of the modes of thought, action, and innovation of the Andean Amazonian peoples, and for acquainting students with other cultures. They are "spaces for intercultural confidence," or places for intercultural mutual nurturance. Their objectives are:

1. To affirm community youth in their own cultural values by reflecting on their role in the nurturance of the Andean Amazonian territories and the cultures they shelter.
2. To provide the space for the understanding, from their position as young community members, of the challenges brought about by modernization of the Andean Amazonian region.
3. To recreate *in situ*, an experience of intercultural relations with young people from other cultures.

Three such schools have been designed thus far: the School of Biodiversity and Food Sufficiency (BFS), the School of Community Skills (CS), and the School of Intercultural Dialogue (ID).

1. School of Biodiversity and Food Sufficiency

This school takes place in the form of visits to communities and short or extended stays in forests and by rivers. It is learning by doing in forests, rivers, and *chacras*. It is oriented to experiencing biodiversity and the local indigenous cosmovision as lived by the organizations of women and elders, nurturers of *chacra*, rivers, and forests. Four kinds of activities take place in this school: learning by living in the biodiversity of the forest and the chacra, the practice of hunting which is understood as trimming the forest, the trimming of the river by fishing, and learning about medicinal plants and the spirits of the forest.

2. School of Community Skills (Crafts)

This school is offered under the modality of workshops conducted by elders, men, and women in the local skills: medicine, weaving, pottery, basket-weaving, cooking, music, singing and dancing. It takes place in the community, the forest, and other appropriate places where the *yachaq*, or community elders, gather to share their knowledge with the young generations. Workshops invite hands-on experience, connecting the young with the elders for the purpose of developing the manual skills of the young, deepening the intergenerational exchange, and producing culturally useful things for the community.

3. School for Intercultural Dialogue

The school for intercultural dialogue is oriented to generate a space for reflection on the Andean Amazonian cultures and peoples, and the role that the young Andean Amazonian community members have in the maintenance of ecological harmony, particularly the relationship of respect between humans and nature. The purpose of the school is to affirm the young in their culture while stimulating their understanding of globalization and its challenges to the community's good living.

Intercultural dialogues take place in a meeting center, schools, or other places appropriate for reflective dialogue. They consist of three modules:

1. Andean Amazonian culture and agriculture;
2. The cultural specificity of indigenous youth in the maintenance of ecological balance; and
3. The effects of extractive industries on indigenous populations and territories, the rights and duties of indigenous peoples, and Earth Jurisprudence.

Contents are developed through group discussions, lectures, presentations, viewing audiovisual materials, and plenary sessions.

MODALITIES OF LEARNING

1. Stays for Intercultural Learning (SIL)

The Stays for Intercultural Learning constitute a modality of learning for urban and rural young people through experiencing relationships of intergenerational respect between *yachaq* and youth. They take place in the *chacra*, the forests, the rivers and lakes, and in the communities where members of different generations meet to learn the peasant crafts and the secrets of conserving biodiversity. In general, those who learn stay in the home of the *yachaq*. This is also the privileged modality in the schools of biodiversity and crafts.

2. *Workshops for Intercultural Learning (WIL)*

These workshops constitute a privileged modality in the school for intercultural dialogue. It includes a sequence of interactions that generally starts with a short presentation on the proposed subject, a previous reading of summaries, a video presentation, group work and plenaries to present the results of the group work and debates. The use of audiovisual material is privileged. Readings are kept short—not exceeding two pages—but are non-trivial, with a format combining written material with drawings and graphs to make the text meaningful in an oral tradition. The two functions of the written material are:

1. The familiarization of the young with the official language—Spanish—in which dialogue with state and corporations is being carried out; and
2. To meet the community's demand that the young must be familiar with two kinds of knowledge: that of their own culture, and the official knowledge taught at schools. Familiarity with the modern requires mastery of the written word.

Analyses of selected texts are done in workshops where youth recreate the intercultural dialogue with others. Performing what is in the texts is presently the privileged approach. Our brief experience thus far attests to the young people's ability to engage in dialogues on diverse subjects with a pertinent intercultural content.

The three schools (crafts, biodiversity, and intercultural dialogue) are closely interwoven. In the schools of crafts and biodiversity, one learns by doing, but at the same time learning offers examples for the reflection on cosmovisions that take place in the School for Intercultural Dialogue. Theory and practice go along together in a relationship of conversation. The schools lead to a UniVida diploma as "intercultural promoter" (or "conmoter," as Gustavo Esteva's puts it).

It is expected that the initiatives of youth organizations in each region may modify their participation in the regeneration of nature in two aspects:

1. In the affirmation of their identity as indigenous peoples living within peasant communities; and
2. In learning to communicate their demands as ethnic groups when dealing with the state and corporations.

An Example of Modules of the School for Intercultural Dialogue

MODULE	SUBJECT	VIDEO
ANDEAN AMAZONIAN AGRICULTURE, FOOD SUFFICIENCY, AND CLIMATE CRISIS	} Andean Amazonian peasant agriculture } Peasant organization and Andean Amazonian organicity } Climate crisis and nurturing water } Climate and climate change } Food sovereignty and Andean Amazonian *micuna*	} *Mama Kawsay Runa Sapichiq* } Modern industrial agriculture } The songs of water } Water pollution } *Puchka Kururay* } Andean Amazonian food culture
FORESTS, WATER, AND *CHACRA*: THE QUECHUA LAMAS LIFE WORLD	} The forest in the Quechua lamas' life world } Water in the Quechua lamas' life world } Quechua lamas' organicity } Quechua lamas' agriculture } Quechua lamas' food	} *Sacha* } *Sembrar para comer* } *El frejol en la vivencia quechua-lamas*
GLOBALIZATION AND THE RIGHTS OF INDIGENOUS PEOPLES	} Globalization and cultural affirmation } Rights of the indigenous peoples	} *¿Acaso comemos plata?* } *Tambogrande* } *Los caminos de todos* } *La historia de las cosas* } *Alimentos transgénicos* } *El cuento de la buena soja*
YOUTH AND CULTURAL REGENERATION	} The role of youth in today's world } To be young. *Warmakay* } UniVida and the nurturing of rural youth } *Iskay Yachay / Paya Yatiwi* or learning two kinds of knowledge in the school	} *Iskay Yachay*

The objective is to influence the regional and national public policies regarding rural youth (the National Youth Policy) and the destinies of the indigenous and peasant communities in the Andes and Amazonia. However, and independent of these impacts, what is crucial in UniVida is the regeneration of the human communities in consonance with the rhythms of nature, and the role that elders have in the regenerative dynamics of the peoples of primordial culture.

The Way Ahead: The Case for Making Wisdom Walk

The regional program, Titikaka (2008–2010), named after the region around Lake Titikaka on the border between Bolivia and Perú, is oriented to the recovery of the relationships that wove a federation among the communities that settled around the sacred lake. The region is recognized as the one with the highest agro-biodiversity on the planet, both in terms of species diversity and the intraspecific variability of cultivated plants. This diversity is closely interlinked with cultural diversity. They go together with the millenary culture of nurturance embodied in the communities of peasant nurturers. The peasant nurturers are ancestors of the present *Suma Uta* network, bearers of an ancient knowledge that secures the sustainable enjoyment of such agro-biodiversity. The program's general objective is to revitalize the multiple and changing paths that seeds have followed in the Perú-Bolivia altiplano since times immemorial, carried by communities of nurturers of agro-biodiversity who have exchanged visits, weaving harmonious ways of living in their places, while learning from each other. Succinctly expressed, the program concept is "Making wisdom walk" and is inspired by the *campesino* concept of the dynamics of seed regeneration in the Andes and the processes that make it possible: the seed paths. (Ishizawa, 2006)

In the In Situ and the Children & Biodiversity projects we found evidence that it is the cosmovision of affection and respect between all entities in the local world, or *pacha*, that conserves agro-biodiversity. The loss of a cultivar is, according to *campesino* testimonies, due to the lack of affection and respect toward the seeds. This feeling of not being cared for makes the seeds look for other more welcoming places, where they will be well received. The local space of seed regeneration is the *ayllu*, the Andean extended family that includes deities and natural entities— along with the human community living in a locality. This is a space of affection and respect that is nurtured in ritual conversation. The organicity of this dynamic is expressed in the system of traditional authorities of the *chacra*, or cultivated field, and the *sallqa*, or wild, giving expression to local forms of governance for keeping the harmony of the *pacha*, or locality.

The extension of this organicity to other places follows the seed paths, which are, viewed over time, ritual regions where the seeds nurture the communities—and are nurtured by them. Within these temporarily delimited ritual spaces a dynamic order is established in which local governance is exercised with affection and respect.

The connections affected by walking the seed paths result in a living web made by the visits that the communities from different *pachas* exchange in the course of the agricultural cycle. They traverse these paths carrying their seeds and their knowledge and then bringing back the knowledge of the host community to be recreated at home.

Characteristic of Promising Processes

1. The *yachaqs* of the participating communities undertake the commitments of a process of cultural affirmation, in particular and foremost, the recovery of their governance system which is based on the traditional concept of authority;
2. Skilled cultural mediators accompany the process of cultural affirmation in the communities and promote the interlinkage of communities; and
3. External resources are made available to the community groups involved in facilitating the re-creation of customs no longer practiced in the community but proved vitally important in host communities.

The program rests on the conviction that the wisdom underlying the Andean nurturance of plants, animals, and the local landscape, as expressed in the communal governance system, has a planetary reach and its exploration may provide valuable suggestions regarding the achievement of good living elsewhere.

Such wisdom is still vital and has been maintained in spite of secular colonization that, during the past half-century, took the form of attempts at modernizing agriculture through the application of technical innovations. The program is based on the wisdom of the *campesino* communities, bearers of the millenary Andean cosmovision whose permanence is a guarantee of sustainability. Also, the agro-biodiversity presently found in the *chacras*, or cultivated fields of the peasant communities, is proof of the pertinence of such knowledge in providing an exemplary and resilient way of life.

The Academic Component

What has become clear from PRATEC's process, since beginning the collection of traditional community practices in the Andes and the inception of the Course on Andean Peasant Agriculture in 1990, is its intellectual character. At first it took the form of developing a coherent discourse on the Andean cosmovision based on the testimonies of its bearers, the peasant nurturers of agro-biodiversity. This endeavor was necessary for us, as we were technical people trained to respect disciplinary boundaries, and since the practices could not be understood as techniques by themselves but only within the context of the life-world. The practices involved the whole community of life, including the diverse life of all communities. Very early on, this implied the simultaneous suspension of:

1. The division of intellectual areas of expertise based on the rigorous practice of disciplines; this was understood as a process of deprofessionalization; and
2. The dominance of the scientific method as the sole criterion of academic rigor, which amounted to a decolonization of the mind.

This led to the development of knowledge relevant to the cultural affirmation of the Andean Amazonian peoples, but deferred the question of engaging in a conversation with the Western techno-scientific tradition.

It is no longer possible to continue without taking on this crucial question. *Iskay Yachay / Paya Yatiwi*, the communities' radical demand for cultural diversity means the nurturance of two kinds of knowledge. The hopeful side of the challenge is that the *yachaqs* are not saying: "You technical experts, solve this for us." They are solving their own problems, dealing with them daily in the many forms that colonization, in the garb of globalization, imposes on our lands. The identification of the root cause of the climate crisis as being the loss of respect towards nature, deities, and among humans, is one example of their approach to setting up an intellectual agenda. For us, it is an invitation to go back to basics, to debating the uncontested ideals of modernity by reminding ourselves of the meaning of sustainable living for each culture, while facing a global challenge that calls for respecting and nurturing diversity. It is an invitation for a decolonizing attitude that accepts the place of the intellectual exercise within a holistic undertaking.

The climate crisis appears to be a wonderful opportunity to see *Iskay Yachay / Paya Yatiwi* in action. Techno-science is able to tell us what we have been doing that is not right and should not do, but local or traditional knowledge is telling us what the root cause of the situation is—and suggesting what should be done to alleviate the climate crisis. Building bridges between levels (global to local) and epistemologies is a formidable academic challenge. And yet, that will not be enough. The specific question for us is whether academics will give up their part of academic imperialism that five centuries ago made Erasmus of Rotterdam refer to professors in the harshest of words. According to Bertrand Russell, Erasmus claimed that "Almost all professors of the arts and sciences are egregiously conceited, and derive their happiness from their conceit." (1946, p. 535).

CHAPTER 10

Concluding Remarks

The revitalization of ecological intelligence within the Peruvian Andes, which is being replicated in other parts of the world by indigenous cultures that have not been entirely overwhelmed by the West's approach to development and formal education, might appear to the casual reader as a model that the Anglo/European cultures in North America should try to emulate. This would be a mistake for several reasons. The first being that the recursive patterns of thinking that have shaped the West's approach to individualism and material progress, and the role of university-trained experts who have a deep bias against the importance of local knowledge, are so widely taken for granted that suggesting that the indigenous cultures of Peru provide a model that should be emulated would lead to even greater expressions of political extremism. The second reason is that any attempt to copy another culture's path of development would divert us from giving close attention to our own community-centered traditions that continue to be sites where intergenerational knowledge of sustainable living practices are still passed along. What we can learn from the indigenous cultures, both in Peru and elsewhere, is the importance of youth learning the knowledge and skills that sustain the local cultural commons that reduce dependence upon a money/consumer-oriented culture. But it will be the knowledge, skills, and patterns of mutual support that represent the genuine ecologically sustainable achievements of western cultures, including the civil liberties as understood in the West, the rights of minority groups, and the possibility of achieving educational reforms that encourage reconstituting our guiding conceptual frameworks that Bateson claims have put us on the pathway of development that is degrading the natural systems upon which we depend.

Our situation is different from that of the indigenous cultures of the Peruvian Andes in anther way. They have a long history of being exploited by western powers and thus have survived by giving close attention to the renewal of their community's ecological intelligence—

which was necessary for maintaining a subsistence level of existence. The messianic tendencies within western cultures—in the sciences, education, technology, free-markets, and humanistic ideals—have been, and still are, driven by a deeply held sense of cultural superiority; and this sense of superiority has made it appear unnecessary to give serious attention to the points Bateson makes about the misconceptions underlying our approach to knowledge, to how our metaphorical language reproduces the hubris and other errors of the past, and to the failure of our educational systems to promote a continual examination of what needs to be conserved and what needs to be radically changed in light of the ecological crisis.

There is another difference that makes unique the challenge we face as a culture. Technological developments, along with our deeply held view of ourselves as autonomous individuals who are impatient with achieving long-term goals (which is now magnified by computer-based technologies), have created a personality type that wants quick explanations of the problems we face and the solutions for fixing them—which now carries over into the realm of politics where instant explanations and criticisms are the norm of the day. Not every aspect of Bateson's thinking lends itself to being understood by this trigger-quick mental attitude. The history of our many misconceptions about the nature of language, individualism, the nature and importance of the cultural and natural commons, and the progressive and supposed cultural neutrality of computer technology cannot be adequately understood by listening to a short talk or reading a brief article. Nor can the alternatives to the cultural practices based on these misconceptions be understood to the point where their sustainable alternatives can be recognized, as they are practiced by people and groups that exist more on the margins of the consumer/industrial culture.

The education acquired during the last fifty years of the twentieth century by classroom teachers, university professors, people who control the media, advertising and corporate executives, and politicians continues to be a major obstacle. But there are signs that there is a recovery of the ecological intelligence that has continued to exist on the margins of our hyper-consumer culture. Organic gardens, non-industrial approaches to raising animals and preserving food, increased reliance upon herbal medicines, the growing interest in participating in the community's creative arts and the recovery of local traditions of craft knowledge and skills, volunteerism, the efforts to promote social and eco-justice awareness, and the vigor that now characterizes the protection of what remains of the environmental commons should be understood as having the same potential for educating youth that the UniVida approach to education has in Peru. The revitalization of ecological intelligence within our local communities needs to be integrated more directly with the efforts to introduce Level III thinking into our public schools and universities—as the examination of our guiding cultural assumptions, the abstractions that are the legacy of our print-oriented culture, and the role that language plays in reproducing the misconceptions of earlier eras (to cite three examples) are otherwise not likely to occur in the conversations and daily activities of the local cultural commons.

References

Abrams, David. 1996. *Spell of the Sensuous: Perception and Language in a More-Than-Human World*. New York: Vintage.

Apffel-Marglin, Frederique, with PRATEC (editors). 1998. *The Spirit of Regeneration: Andean Culture Confronting Western Notions of Development*. London: Zed Books.

Asociación Bartolome Aripaylla. 2001. *Kawsay, Kawsaymama: La Regeneracion de semillas en los Andes Centrales del Peru*. Ayacucho, Peru: Asociación Bartolome Aripaylla.

Ayers, William, Theresa Quine, and David Stovall (editors). 2009. *Handbook of Social Justice in Education*. New York: Routledge.

Basso, Keith. 1996. *Wisdom Sits in Places: Landscape and Language Among the Western Apache*. Albuquerque, N.M.: University of New Mexico Press.

Bateson, Gregory. 1936. *Naven: A Survey of the Problems Suggested by a Composite Picture of the Culture of a New Guinea Tribe*. Cambridge, G.B.: University of Cambridge Press.

Bateson, Gregory. 1972. *Steps to an Ecology of Mind*. New York: Ballantine Books.

Bateson, Gregory. 1979. *Mind and Nature: A Necessary Unity*. New York: Bantam Books.

Bateson, Gregory. 1991. *A Sacred Unity: Further Steps to an Ecology of Mind*. New York: A Cornelia & Michael Bessie Book.

Bateson, Gregory, and Mary Catherine Bateson. 1987. *Angels Fear: Towards an Epistemology of the Sacred*. New York: Macmillan Publishing Co.

Bowers, C.A. 1995. *Educating for an Ecologically Sustainable Culture: Rethinking Moral Education, Creativity, Intelligence, and Other Modern Orthodoxies.* New York: New York University Press.

Bowers, C.A. 2000. *Let Them Eat Data: How Computers Affect Education, Cultural Diversity, and the Prospects for Ecological Sustainability.* Athens, Ga.: University of Georgia Press.

Bowers, C.A. 2008. *Toward a Post-Industrial Consciousness: Understanding the Linguistic Basis of Ecologically Sustainable Educational Reforms.* www.cabowers.net

Bowers, C.A. 2009. *Educating for Ecological Intelligence.* www.cabowers.net

Bowers, C.A. 2011. *Essays on Ecologically Sustainable Educational Reforms.* www.cabowers.net

Buber, Martin. 1955. *Between Man and Man.* Boston: Beacon Press.

Bury, J. B. 1932. *The Idea of Progress: An Inquiry into its Growth and Origins.* New York: Dover Publications.

Calvin, John. 1634. *Institution of Christian Religion.* London: Norton and Whitaker.

Capra, Fritjof. 1996. *The Web of Life: A New Scientific Understanding of Living Systems.* New York: Anchor Books.

Carson, Rachel. 1962. *Silent Spring.* New York: Fawcett Crest.

Chomsky, Noam. 1989. *Necessary Illusions: Thought Control in Democratic Societies.* London: Pluto Press.

Chomsky, Noam. 1992. *Deterring Democracy.* London: Vintage.

Chomsky, Noam and Edward S. Herman. 1994. *Manufacturing Consent: The Political Economy of the Mass Media.* London: Vintage.

Cutipa Flores, Juan Arturo. 2006. "La Percepción del Clima por las Familias Aymaras" (Discussion paper), Puno, Peru: Asociación Chuyma Aru.

Daly, Herman E. 1996. "Consumption: Value Added, Physical Transformation, and Welfare." In *Getting Down to Earth: Practical Applications of Ecological Economics*, edited by Robert Costanza, Olman Segura, and Juan Martinez-Alier. Washington, D. C.: Island Press, 49–59.

Dreyfus, Hubert L. and Paul Rabinow. 1982. *Michel Foucault: Beyond Structuralism and Hermeneutics*. Chicago: University of Chicago Press.

Fernandez-Armsto, Felipe. 2000. *Civilizations*. London: Pan Books.

Freire, Paulo. 1971. *Pedagogy of the Oppressed*. New York: Herder and Herder.

Goleman, Daniel. 2009. *Ecological Intelligence: How Knowing the Hidden Impacts of What We Buy Can Change Everything*. New York: Broadway Books.

Goody, Jack. 1987. *The Interface Between the Written and the Oral*. Cambridge, U.K.: Cambridge University Press.

Goody, Jack. 2000. *The Power of the Written Tradition*. Washington, D.C.: Smithsonian Institution Press.

Gouldner, Alvin. 1979. *The Future of Intellectuals and the Rise of the New Class*. New York: Seabury Press.

Harries-Jones, Peter. 1995. *A Recursive Vision: Ecological Understanding and Gregory Bateson*. Toronto: University of Toronto Press.

Hartmann, T. 2001. *The Last Hours of Ancient Sunlight*. London: Hodder & Stoughton.

Havelock, Eric A. 1986. *The Muse Learns to Write: Reflections on Orality and Literacy from Antiquity to the Present*. New Haven, Conn.: Yale University Press.

Hedges, Chris. 2010. "Zero Point of Systemic Collapse." In *Adbusters*, Vol. 18, No. 2 (March/April), 88.

The Invisible Committee. 2007. *The Coming Insurrection*.
   http://tarnac9.wordpress.com/texts/the-coming-insurrection/
   (originally published in French by La fabrique editions).
   Accessed 26 February 2010.

Ishizawa, Jorge. 2006. "Cosmovisions and Environmental Governance." In *Bridging Scales and Knowledge Systems: Concepts and
   Applications in Ecosystem Assessment*, edited by Walker V. Reid,
   et al. New York: Island Press.

Ishizawa, Jorge, and Grimaldo Rengifo. 2009. "Biodiversity
   Regeneration and Intercultural Knowledge Transmission in the
   Peruvian Andes." In *Learning and Knowing in Indigenous Societies
   Today*, edited by Peter Bates, et al. Paris: UNESCO.

Jucker, Rolf. 2002. "Our Common Illiteracy: Education as if the
   Earth and People Mattered." In *Environmental Education,
   Communication and Sustainability*, Vol. 10. Frankfurt; Berlin;
   Bern; Bruxelles; New York; Oxford; Wien: Lang Accessible at:
   http://books.google.de/books?id=whJ_AAAAMAAJ&source=gbs_
   navlinks_s.

Jucker, Rolf. 2003. "UNESCO's Teaching and Learning for a
   Sustainable Future: A critical evaluation of underlying unsustainable progress myths." In *The Trumpeter*, Vol. 19, No. 2, 83–107.
   Accessible at: http://trumpeter.athabascau.ca/index.php/trumpet/
   article/view/92/95].

Jucker, Rolf. 2008. "EcoJustice Education: Communal Learning
   Beyond Capitalism." In *The EcoJustice Review*, Educating for the
   Commons. (May, 2008). Accessible at: http://www.ecojusticeedu-
   cation.org/index.php?option=com_content&task=view&id=62&
   Itemid=44 or http://www.ecojusticeeducation.org/images/stories/
   Articles_Extras/rolf_jucker_article.pdf, accessed 2 March 2010.

Jucker, Rolf. (forthcoming). *ESD Between Systemic Change and
   Bureaucratic Obfuscation. Some reflections on Environmental
   Education and Education for Sustainable Development in
   Switzerland*. Manuscript.

Künzli David, Christine. 2007. *Zukunft mitgestalten—Bildung für eine nachhaltige Entwicklung—Didaktisches Konzept und Umsetzung in der Grundschule.* Bern, Stuttgart, Wien: Haupt.

Kyburz-Graber, Regula (editor). 2006. *Kompetenzen für die Zukunft.* Nachhaltige Entwicklung konkret. Bern: h.e.p. Verlag.

Lakoff, George, and Mark Johnson. 1999. *Philosophy in the Flesh: The Embodied Mind and its Challenge to Western Thought.* New York: Basic Books.

Lansing, Stephen J. 1991. *Priests and Programmers: Technologies of Power in the Engineered Landscape of Bali.* Princeton, N.J.: Princeton University Press.

Leopold. Aldo. 1960. *A Sand County Almanac: And Sketches from Here and There.* New York: Oxford University Press.

Maturana, Humberto, and Gloria Guiloff. 1980. "The Quest for the Intelligence of Intelligence." In *Journal of Social Biological Structures*, Vol. 3, 135–148. London: Academic Press.

MacIntyre, Alasdair. 1984. *After Virtue: A Study in Moral Theory.* Notre Dame, Ind.: University of Notre Dame Press.

Marshall, Peter. 1993. *Demanding the Impossible: A History of Anarchism.* London: Fontana Press.

Martin, Hans-Peter and Harald Schumann. 1997. *The Global Trap: Globalization and the assault on prosperity and democracy,* translated by Patrick Camiller. London; New York: Zed Books.

OECD. 2005. *The Definition and Selection of key Competencies.* Executive Summary. Paris: OECD. Accessible at www.oecd.org/dataoecd/47/61/35070367.pdf

Ong, Walter. 1982. *Orality and Literacy: The Technologizing of the Word.* London: Methuen.

Platform for Agrobiodiversity Research. 2010. "The Use of Agrobiodiversity by Indigenous and Traditional Agricultural Communities." In *Adapting to Climate Change.* Rome: PAR.

PRATEC. 1993. *Afirmacion Cultural Andina*. Lima: PRATEC.

PRATEC. 2010. "La Experiencia del Fondo Iniciativas de Afirmacion Cultural" (FICA) 2002–2009: 3 *Crianza del Clima en los Andes Centrales*. Lima: PRATEC.

Rand, Ayn. 1964. *The Virtue of Selfishness: A New Concept of Egoism*. New York: Penguin.

Reddy, Michael. J. 1979. "The Conduit Metaphor—A Case of Frame Conflict in Our Language About Language." In *Metaphor and Thought*, edited by Andrew Ortony. Cambridge, G. B.: Cambridge University Press, 284–323.

Rengifo, Vasquez, Grimaldo. 2008. *Educación y Diversidad Cultural: 4 Los Oficios Campesinos*. Lima: PRATEC.

Rockström, J., W. Steffen, K. Noone, Å. Persson, F.S. Chapin, III, E. Lambin, T.M. Lenton, M. Scheffer, C. Folke, H. Schellnhuber, B. Nykvist, C.A. De Wit, T. Hughes, S. van der Leeuw, H. Rodhe, S. Sörlin, P.K. Snyder, R. Costanza, U. Svedin, M. Falkenmark, L. Karlberg, R.W. Corell, V.J. Fabry, J. Hansen, B. Walker, D. Liverman, K. Richardson, P. Crutzen, and J. Foley (2009): "Planetary Noundaries: Exploring the Safe Operating Space for Humanity." In *Ecology and Society*, Volume 14, Issue 2, Article 32. Accessible at: www.ecologyandsociety.org/vol14/iss2/art32/ or www.ecologyandsociety.org/vol14/iss2/art32/ES-2009-3180.pdf Accessed 26 February 2010.

Ross, Rupert. 1996. *Return to the Teachings: Exploring Aboriginal Justice*. Toronto: Penguin.

Russell, Bertrand. 1946. *A History of Western Philosophy*. London: George Allen and Urwin.

Sachs, Wolfgang. 1999. *Planet Dialectics. Explorations in Environment and Development*. London: Zed Books.

Sale, Kirkpatrick. 1995. *Rebels Against the Future: The Luddites and Their War Against the Industrial Revolution*. Reading, Mass.: Addison-Wesley.

Selby, David. 2007. "As the heating happens: Education for Sustainable Development or Education for Sustainable Contraction?" In *International Journal of Innovation and Sustainable Development*, Vol. 2, No. 3/4: 249–267.

Sennett, Richard. 2008. *The Craftsman*. New Haven, Conn.: Yale University Press.

Shiva, Vandana. 2005. *Earth Democracy: Justice, Sustainability, and Peace*. Cambridge, Mass.: South End Press.

Simlife. 1995. Orinda, Calif.: Maxis.

Simms, Andrew and Victoria Johnson. 2010. *Growth isn't possible. Why we need a new economic direction*. London: nef (new economics foundation). Download at: www.neweconomics.org/sites/neweconomics.org/files/Growth_Isnt_Possible.pdf Accessed 26 February 2010.

Smith, Adam. 1937. *An Inquiry into the Nature and Causes of the Wealth of Nations*. New York: Modern Library.

Smith, Adam. 1976. *Theory of Moral Sentiments*. Oxford, G. B.: Clarendon Press.

Snyder, Gary. 1990. *The Practice of the Wild*. San Francisco, Calif.: North Point Press.

Terra des hommes—Germany. 2001. *Children and Biodiversity in the Andes*. Lima: terre des hommes—Germany.

UNESCO. 2005. *United Nations Decade of Education for Sustainable Development (2005–2014): Guidelines and Recommendations for Reorienting Teacher Education to Address Sustainability*. Paris: UNESCO (Education for Sustainable Development in Action Technical Paper No. 2). http://unesdoc.unesco.org/images/0014/001433/143370E.pdf Accessed 1 March 2010.

UNESCO. 2009. *United Nations Decade of Education for Sustainable Development (DESD, 2005–2014) Review of Contexts and Structures for Education for Sustainable Development 2009*. Written by Arjen Wals. Paris: UNESCO.

United Nations. 1998. *Universal Declaration of Human Rights.*
    Geneva: UN. http://www.un.org/en/documents/udhr/
    Accessed 2 March 2010.

*Zukunftsfähiges Deutschland in einer globalisierten Welt. Ein Anstoss
    zur gesellschaftlichen Debatte.* 2008. Edited by BUND and
    Brot für eine Welt, written by Wuppertal Institut für Klima,
    Umwelt, Energie, lead author Wolfgang Sachs. Frankfurt:
    Fischer Taschenbuch.

About the Contributors

C.A. (Chet) Bowers received his Ph.D. from the University of California. He left graduate school with an interdisciplinary understanding of the history of educational reform and social thought and with an awareness that most of his graduate studies failed to address how western traditions in philosophy and political theory were based on colonizing and ecologically problematic cultural assumptions. Over the years he has written 21 books that address the silences and misconceptions that continue to marginalize awareness of the cultural, and thus educational, roots of the ecological crisis. He has been an invited speaker at 33 American universities and 37 universities in Europe, Asia, Australia, South Africa, Canada, and South America. He is now semi-retired and continues to write and speak internationally.

Jorge Ishizawa has devoted his professional career to socio-economic planning, both in the Peruvian public administration and in international organizations. Since 1996 he has been a member of the Proyecto Andino de Tecnologías Campesinas (PRATEC), a non-governmental organization whose mission is the cultural affirmation of the Andean Amazonian communities, based on their own knowledge and traditions. Presently he is also a member of the newly founded Complex Thought Institute of Ricardo Palma University. He is based in Lima.

Rolf Jucker is director of the Swiss Foundation for Environmental Education which is responsible for integrating environmental education into the Swiss educational system. He has a masters degree in education for sustainability (EIS), is an international advisor on EIS-based educational reforms, and has published widely on the subject (see rolfjucker.net). His book, *Our Common Illiteracy: Education as if the Earth and People Mattered,* was published in 2002.

Grimaldo Rengifo holds a degree in education from the Universidad Nacional del Centro Huancayo in Peru. He also earned an anthropology diploma from the Catholic University of Peru. He founded the Proyecto Andino de Tecnologías Campesinas (PRATEC) in 1986 and is its present coordinator. Before founding PRATEC he held various posts in government and in international organizations. He is the author of numerous books and essays.

Acknowledgments

While my name may be the principal one associated with the title of this book, it is necessary to acknowledge that the main focus of the book, as well as the theoretical frameworks that inform both the analysis and recommendations for educational reforms, were influenced by many others. I have drawn heavily upon the thinking of a wide range of scholars who have deepened my understanding of the recursive cultural patterns that have marginalized awareness of environmental limits and the traditions of community self-sufficiency. The most prominent sources of influence include Jacques Ellul, Eric Havelock, Walter Ong, Ron Scollon, Karl Polanyi, Clifford Geertz, Michael Oakeshott, Edmund Burke, and Edward Shils. Influential environmental thinkers include Aldo Leopold, Wendell Berry, and Vandana Shiva, as well as the other members of the deep ecology discussion group who, over a period of four years, introduced me to Third World perspectives on issues of sustainable cultural practices and local resistance to economic globalization.

Colleagues, as well as students in different parts of the world, have shared their efforts to promote many of the reforms that have become central to my thinking. Their suggestions have expanded my thinking about how to relate reform proposals to different cultural contexts and to different ideological sources of resistance. In effect, they influenced me to become a more context-oriented thinker and to be constantly aware of differences in cultural ways of knowing. Their insights helped me to avoid one of the problems of putting ideas into print, a medium which too often turns ideas into universal prescriptions for how to introduce reforms. Learning from colleagues and former students has also been a source of encouragement that my work has not been completely overtaken by the spread of a cultural amnesia that seems to accompany the adoption of today's consciousness-changing technologies.

I owe a special debt of gratitude to my wife, Mary Katharine Bowers, who cheerfully faced the daunting challenge of reading the first draft of the book manuscript and for demanding that I take account of the perspective of readers who might be encountering, for the first time, a radically different way of thinking. For bringing a keen eye to reading the manuscript in its later versions, and for suggesting changes that eliminated conceptual distractions and other problems, I wish to thank Lynn Marx. I also wish to thank David Diethelm for taking on the position of managing director of the Eco-Justice Press and for his commitment to publishing books that address the cultural issues often overlooked when thinking about ecologically sustainable educational reforms.